NO HERO

E. W. HORNUNG

No Hero

E. W. Hornung

© 1st World Library, 2007
PO Box 2211
Fairfield, IA 52556
www.1stworldlibrary.com
First Edition

LCCN: 2007930727

Softcover ISBN: 978-1-4218-4808-2
Hardcover ISBN: 978-1-4218-4711-5
eBook ISBN: 978-1-4218-4905-8

Purchase *"No Hero"*
as a traditional bound book at:
www.1stWorldLibrary.com/purchase.asp?ISBN=978-1-4218-4808-2

1st World Library is a literary, educational organization
dedicated to:

- Creating a free internet library of downloadable ebooks

- Hosting writing competitions and offering book publishing
scholarships.

Interested in more 1st World Library books? contact:
literacy@1stworldlibrary.com

Check us out at: www.1stworldlibrary.com

1ˢᵗ World Library Literary Society

Giving Back to the World

"If you want to work on the core problem, it's early school literacy."

- James Barksdale, former CEO of Netscape

"No skill is more crucial to the future of a child, or to a democratic and prosperous society, than literacy."

- Los Angeles Times

"Literacy... means far more than learning how to read and write... The aim is to transmit... knowledge and promote social participation."

- UNESCO

"Literacy is not a luxury, it is a right and a responsibility. If our world is to meet the challenges of the twenty-first century we must harness the energy and creativity of all our citizens."

- President Bill Clinton

"Parents should be encouraged to read to their children, and teachers should be equipped with all available techniques for teaching literacy, so the varying needs and capacities of individual kids can be taken into account."

- Hugh Mackay

CONTENTS

I. A Plenipotentiary 7

II. The Theatre of War 25

III. First Blood... 35

IV. A Little Knowledge 45

V. A Marked Woman 55

VI. Out of Action 63

VII. Second Fiddle 70

VIII. Prayers and Parables 79

IX. Sub Judice 92

X. The Last Word... 102

XI. The Lion's Mouth... 116

XII. A Stern Chase 128

XIII. Number Three 141

CHAPTER I

A PLENIPOTENTIARY

Has no writer ever dealt with the dramatic aspect of the unopened envelope? I cannot recall such a passage in any of my authors, and yet to my mind there is much matter for philosophy in what is always the expressionless shell of a boundless possibility. Your friend may run after you in the street, and you know at a glance whether his news is to be good, bad, or indifferent; but in his handwriting on the breakfast-table there is never a hint as to the nature of his communication. Whether he has sustained a loss or an addition to his family, whether he wants you to dine with him at the club or to lend him ten pounds, his handwriting at least will be the same, unless, indeed, he be offended, when he will generally indite your name with a studious precision and a distant grace quite foreign to his ordinary caligraphy.

These reflections, trite enough as I know, are nevertheless inevitable if one is to begin one's unheroic story in the modern manner, at the latest possible point. That is clearly the point at which a waiter brought me the fatal letter from Catherine Evers. Apart even from its immediate consequences, the letter had a *prima facie* interest, of no ordinary kind, as the first for years from a once constant correspondent. And so I sat studying the envelope with a curiosity too piquant not to be enjoyed. What in the world could so obsolete a friend find to say to one now? Six months earlier there had been a certain opportunity for an advance, which at that time could not possibly have been misconstrued; when they landed me, a few later, there was another and perhaps a better one. But this was the last summer of the late century, and already I was beginning to get about like a lamplighter on my two sticks. Now, young men about town, on two walking-sticks, in the year of grace 1900, meant only one thing. Quite a stimulating thing in the beginning, but even as I write, in this the next winter but one, a national irritation of which the name alone might prevent you from reading another word.

Catherine's handwriting, on the contrary, was still stimulating, if indeed I ever found it more so in the foolish past. It had not altered in the least. There was the same sweet pedantry of the Attic *e*, the same superiority to the most venial abbreviation, the same inconsistent forest of exclamatory notes, thick as poplars across the channel. The present plantation started after my own Christian name, to wit "Dear Duncan!!" Yet there was nothing Germanic in Catherine's ancestry; it was only her apologetic little way of addressing me as though nothing had ever happened, of asking whether she might. Her own old tact and charm were in that tentative burial of the past. In the first line she had all but won my entire forgiveness; but the very next interfered with the effect.

"You promised to do anything for me!"

I should be sorry to deny it, I am sure, for not to this day do I know what I did say on the occasion to which she evidently referred. But was it kind to break the silence of years with such a reference? Was it even quite decent in Catherine to ignore my existence until I could be of use to her, and then to ask the favour in her first breath? It was true, as she went on to remind me, that we were more or less connected after all, and at least conceivable that no one else could help her as I could, if I would. In any case, it was a certain satisfaction to hear that Catherine herself was of the last opinion. I read on. She was in a difficulty; but she did not say what the difficulty was. For one unworthy moment the thought of money entered my mind, to be ejected the next, as the Catherine of old came more and more into the mental focus. Pride was the last thing in which I had found her wanting, and her letter indicated no change in that respect.

"You may wonder," she wrote just at the end, "why I have never sent you a single word of inquiry, or sympathy, or congratulation!! Well—suppose it was 'bad blood'!! between us when you went away! Mind, *I* never meant it to be so, but suppose it was: could I treat the dear old you like that, and the Great New You like somebody else? You have your own fame to thank for my unkindness! *I* am only thankful they haven't given you the V.C.!! *Then* I should *never* have dared—not even now!!!"

I smoked a cigarette when I had read it all twice over, and as I crushed the fire out of the stump I felt I could as soon think of lighting it again as I should have expected Catherine Evers to set a fresh match to me. That, I was resolved, she should never do; nor was I quite coxcomb enough to suspect her of the desire for a moment. But a man who has once made a fool of himself, especially about a woman somewhat older than himself, does not soon get over the soreness; and mine returned with the very fascination which made itself felt even in the shortest little letter.

Catherine wrote from the old address in Elm Park Gardens, and she wanted me to call as early as I could, or to make any appointment I liked. I therefore telegraphed that I was coming at three o'clock that afternoon, and thus made for myself one of the longest mornings that I can remember spending in town. I was staying at the time at the Kensington Palace Hotel, to be out of the central racket of things, and yet more or less under the eye of the surgeon who still hoped to extract the last bullet in time. I can remember spending half the morning gazing aimlessly over the grand old trees, already prematurely bronzed, and the other half in limping in their shadow to the Round Pond, where a few little townridden boys were sailing their humble craft. It was near the middle of August, and for the first time I was thankful that an earlier migration had not been feasible in my case.

In spite of my telegram Mrs. Evers was not at home when I arrived, but she had left a message which more than explained matters. She was lunching out, but only in Brechin Place, and I was to wait in the study if I did not mind. I did not, and yet I did, for the room in which Catherine certainly read her books and wrote her letters was also the scene of that which I was beginning to find it rather hard work to forget as it was. Nor had it changed any more than her handwriting, or than the woman herself as I confidently expected to find her now. I have often thought that at about forty both sexes stand still to the eye, and I did not expect Catherine Evers, who could barely have reached that rubicon, to show much symptom of the later marches. To me, here in her den, the other year was just the other day. My time in India was little better than a dream to me, while as for angry shots at either end of Africa, it was never I who had been there to hear them. I must have come by my sticks in some less romantic fashion. Nothing could convince me that I had ever been many days or miles away from a room that I knew by heart, and found full as I left it of familiar trifles and poignant associations.

That was the shelf devoted to her poets; there was no

E. W. Hornung

addition that I could see. Over it hung the fine photograph of Watts's "Hope," an ironic emblem, and elsewhere one of that intolerably sad picture, his "Paolo and Francesca": how I remembered the wet Sunday when Catherine took me to see the original in Melbury Road! The old piano which was never touched, the one which had been in St. Helena with Napoleon's doctor, there it stood to an inch where it had stood of old, a sort of grand-stand for the photographs of Catherine's friends. I descried my own young effigy among the rest, in a frame which I recollected giving her at the time. Well, I looked all the idiot I must have been; and there was the very Persian rug that I had knelt on in my idiocy! I could afford to smile at myself to-day; yet now it all seemed yesterday, not even the day before, until of a sudden I caught sight of that other photograph in the place of honour on the mantelpiece. It was one by Hills and Sanders, of a tall youth in flannels, armed with a long-handled racket, and the sweet open countenance which Robin Evers had worn from his cradle upward. I should have known him anywhere and at any age. It was the same dear, honest face; but to think that this giant was little Bob! He had not gone to Eton when I saw him last; now I knew from the sporting papers that he was up at Cambridge; but it was left to his photograph to bring home the flight of time.

Certainly his mother would never have done so when all at once the door opened and she stood before me, looking about thirty in the ample shadow of a cavalier's hat. Simply but admirably gowned, as I knew she would be, her slender figure looked more youthful still; yet in all this there was no intent; the dry cool smile was that of an older woman, and I was prepared for greater cordiality than I could honestly detect in the greeting of the small firm hand. But it was kind, as indeed her whole reception of me was; only it had always been the way of Catherine the correspondent to make one expect a little more than mere kindness, and of Catherine the companion to disappoint that expectation. Her conversation needed few exclamatory points.

"Still halt and lame," she murmured over my sticks. "You poor thing, you are to sit down this instant."

And I obeyed her as one always had, merely remarking that I was getting along famously now.

"You must have had an awful time," continued Catherine, seating herself near me, her calm wise eyes on mine.

"Blood-poisoning," said I. "It nearly knocked me out, but I'm glad to say it didn't quite."

Indeed, I had never felt quite so glad before.

"Ah! that was too hard and cruel; but I was thinking of the day itself," explained Catherine, and paused in some sweet transparent awe of one who had been through it.

"It was a beastly day," said I, forgetting her objection to the epithet until it was out. But Catherine did not wince. Her fixed eyes were full of thought.

"It was all that here," she said. "One depressing morning I had a telegram from Bob, 'Spion Kop taken'—"

"So Bob," I nodded, "had it as badly as everybody else!"

"Worse," declared Catherine, her eye hardening; "it was all I could do to keep him at Cambridge, though he had only just gone up. He would have given up everything and flown to the Front if I had let him."

And she wore the inexorable face with which I could picture

E. W. Hornung

her standing in his way; and in Catherine I could admire that dogged look and all it spelt, because a great passion is always admirable. The passion of Catherine's life was her boy, the only son of his mother, and she a widow. It had been so when he was quite small, as I remembered it with a pinch of jealousy startling as a twinge from an old wound. More than ever must it be so now; that was as natural as the maternal embargo in which Catherine seemed almost to glory. And yet, I reflected, if all the widows had thought only of their only sons—and of themselves!

"The next depressing morning," continued Catherine, happily oblivious of what was passing through one's mind, "the first thing I saw, the first time I put my nose outside, was a great pink placard with 'Spion Kop Abandoned!' Duncan, it was too awful."

"I wish we'd sat tight," I said, "I must confess."

"Tight!" cried Catherine in dry horror. "I should have abandoned it long before. I should have run away—hard! To think that you didn't—that's quite enough for me."

And again I sustained the full flattery of that speechless awe which was yet unembarrassing by reason of its freedom from undue solemnity.

"There were some of us who hadn't a leg to run on," I had to say; "I was one, Mrs. Evers."

"I beg your pardon?"

"Catherine, then." But it put me to the blush.

"Thank you. If you really wish me to call you 'Captain Clephane' you have only to say so; but in that case I can't ask the favour I had made up my mind to ask—of so old a friend."

Her most winning voice was as good a servant as ever; the touch of scorn in it was enough to stimulate, but not to sting; and it was the same with the sudden light in the steady intellectual eyes.

"Catherine," I said, "you can't indeed ask any favour of me! There you are quite right. It is not a word to use between us."

Mrs. Evers gave me one of her deliberate looks before replying.

"And I am not so sure that it is a favour," she said softly enough at last. "It is really your advice I want to ask, in the first place at all events. Duncan, it's about old Bob!"

The corners of her mouth twitched, her eyes filled with a quaint humorous concern, and as a preamble I was handed the photograph which I had already studied on my own account.

"Isn't he a dear?" asked Bob's mother. "Would you have known him, Duncan?"

"I did know him," said I. "Spotted him at a glance. He's the same old Bob all over."

I was fortunate enough to meet the swift glance I got for that, for in sheer sweetness and affection it outdid all remembered glances of the past. In a moment it was as though I had more than regained the lost ground of lost years. And in another moment, on the heels of the discovery, came the still more startling one that I was glad to have regained my ground, was thankful to be reinstated, and strangely, acutely, yet

E. W. Hornung

uneasily happy, as I had never been since the old days in this very room.

Half in a dream I heard Catherine telling of her boy, of his Eton triumphs, how he had been one of the rackets pair two years, and in the eleven his last, but "in Pop" before he was seventeen, and yet as simple and unaffected and unspoilt with it all as the small boy whom I remembered. And I did remember him, and knew his mother well enough to believe it all; for she did not chant his praises to organ music, but rather hummed them to the banjo; and one felt that her own demure humour, so signal and so permanent a charm in Catherine, would have been the saving of half-a-dozen Bobs.

"And yet," she wound up at her starting-point, "it's about poor old Bob I want to speak to you!"

"Not in a fix, I hope?"

"I hope not, Duncan."

Catherine was serious now.

"Or mischief?"

"That depends on what you mean by mischief."

Catherine was more serious still.

"Well, there are several brands, but only one or two that really poison—unless, of course, a man is very poor."

And my mind harked back to its first suspicion, of some financial embarrassment, now conceivable enough; but Catherine told me her boy was not poor, with the air of one who would have drunk ditchwater rather than let the other want for champagne.

"It is just the opposite," she added: "in little more than a year, when he comes of age, he will have quite as much as is good for him. You know what he is, or rather you don't. I do. And if I were not his mother I should fall in love with him myself!"

Catherine looked down on me as she returned from replacing Bob's photograph on the mantelpiece. The humour had gone out of her eye; in its place was an almost animal glitter, a far harder light than had accompanied the significant reference to the patriotic impulse which she had nipped in the bud. It was probably only the old, old look of the lioness whose whelp is threatened, but it was something new to me in Catherine Evers, something half-repellent and yet almost wholly fine.

"You don't mean to say it's that?" I asked aghast.

"No, I don't," Catherine answered, with a hard little laugh. "He's not quite twenty, remember; but I am afraid that he is making a fool of himself, and I want it stopped."

I waited for more, merely venturing to nod my sympathetic concern.

"Poor old Bob, as you may suppose, is not a genius. He is far too nice," declared Catherine's old self, "to be anything so nasty. But I always thought he had his head screwed on, and his heart screwed in, or I never would have let him loose in a Swiss hotel. As it was, I was only too glad for him to go with George Kennerley, who was as good at work at Eton as Bob was at games."

In Catherine's tone, for all the books on her shelves, the

　　　　　E. W. Hornung

pictures on her walls, there was no doubt at all as to which of the two an Eton boy should be good at, and I agreed sincerely with another nod.

"They were to read together for an hour or so every day. I thought it would be a nice little change for Bob, and it was quite a chance; he must do a certain amount of work, you see. Well, they only went at the beginning of the month, and already they have had enough of each other's society."

"You don't mean that they've had a row?"

Catherine inclined a mortified head.

"Bob never had such a thing in his life before, nor did I ever know anybody who succeeded in having one with Bob. It does take two, you know. And when one of the two has an angelic temper, and tact enough for twenty—"

"You naturally blame the other," I put in, as she paused in visible perplexity.

"But I don't, Duncan, and that's just the point. George is devoted to Bob, and is as nice as he can be himself, in his own sober, honest, plodding way. He may not have the temper, he certainly has not the tact, but he worships Bob and has come back quite miserable."

"Then he has come back, and you have seen him?"

"He was here last night. You must know that Bob writes to me every day, even from Cambridge, if it's only a line; and in yesterday's letter he mentioned quite casually that George had had enough of it and was off home. It was a little too casual to be quite natural in old Bob, and there are other things he has been mentioning in the same way. If any instinct is to be relied upon it is a mother's, and mine amounted almost to second sight. I sent Master George a telegram, and he came in last night."

"Well?'"

"Not a word! There was bad blood between them, but that was all I could get out of him. Vulgar disagreeables between Bob, of all people, and his greatest friend! If you could have seen the poor fellow sitting where you are sitting now, like a prisoner in the dock! I put him in the witness-box instead, and examined him on scraps of Bob's letters to me. It was as unscrupulous as you please, but I felt unscrupulous; and the poor dear was too loyal to admit, yet too honest to deny, a single thing."

"And?" said I, as Bob's mother paused again.

"And," cried she, with conscious melodrama in the fiery twinkle of her eye—"and, I know all! There is an odious creature at the hotel—a widow, if you please! A 'ripping widow' Bob called her in his first letter; then it was 'Mrs. Lascelles'; but now it is only 'some people' whom he escorts here, there, and everywhere. *Some* people, indeed!"

Catherine smiled unmercifully. I relied upon my nod.

"I needn't tell you," she went on, "that the creature is at least twenty years older than my baby, and not at all nice at that. George didn't tell me, mind, but he couldn't deny a single thing. It was about her that they fell out. Poor George remonstrated, not too diplomatically, I daresay, but I can quite see that my Bob behaved as he was never known to behave on land or sea. The poor child has been bewitched, neither more nor less."

"He'll get over it," I murmured, with the somewhat shaky confidence born of my own experience.

Catherine looked at me in mild surprise.

"But it's going on now, Duncan—it's going on still!"

"Well," I added, with all the comfort that my voice would carry, and which an exaggerated concern seemed to demand: "well, Catherine, it can't go very far at his age!" Nor to this hour can I yet conceive a sounder saying, in all the circumstances of the case, and with one's knowledge of the type of lad; but my fate was the common one of comforters, and I was made speedily and painfully aware that I had now indeed said the most unfortunate thing.

Catherine did not stamp her foot, but she did everything else required by tradition of the exasperated lady. Not go far? As if it had not gone too far already to be tolerated another instant longer than was necessary!

"He is making a fool of himself—my boy—my Bob—before a whole hotelful of sharp eyes and sharper tongues! Is that not far enough for it to have gone? Duncan, it must be stopped, and stopped at once; but I am not the one to do it. I would rather it went on," cried Catherine tragically, as though the pit yawned before us all, "than that his mother should fly to his rescue before all the world! But a friend might do it, Duncan—if—"

Her voice had dropped. I bent my ear.

"If only," she sighed, "I had a friend who would!"

Catherine was still looking down when I looked up; but the droop of the slender body, the humble angle of the cavalier hat, the faint flush underneath, all formed together a challenge and an appeal which were the more irresistible for their sweet shamefacedness. Acute consciousness of the past (I thought), and (I even fancied) some penitence for a wrong by no means past undoing, were in every sensitive inch of her, as she sat a suppliant to the old player of that part. And there are emotions of which the body may be yet more eloquent than the face; there was the figure of Watts's "Hope" drooping over as she drooped, not more lissom and speaking than her own; just then it caught my eye, and on the spot it was as though the lute's last string of that sweet masterpiece had vibrated aloud in Catherine's room.

My hand shook as I reached for my trusty sticks, but I cannot say that my voice betrayed me when I inquired the name of the Swiss hotel.

"The Riffel Alp," said Catherine—"above Zermatt, you know."

"I start to-morrow morning," I rejoined, "if that will do."

Then Catherine looked up. I cannot describe her look. Transfiguration were the idle word, but the inadequate, and yet more than one would scatter the effect of so sudden a burst of human sunlight.

"Would you really go?" she cried. "Do you mean it, Duncan?"

"I only wish," I replied, "that it were to Australia."

"But then you would be weeks too late."

"Ah, that's another story! I may be too late as it is."

Her brightness clouded on the instant; only a gleam of annoyance pierced the cloud.

"Too late for what, may I ask?"

"Everything except stopping the banns."

"Please don't talk nonsense, Duncan. Banns at nineteen!"

"It is nonsense, I agree; at the same time the minor consequences will be the hardest to deal with. If they are being talked about, well, they are being talked about. You know Bob best: suppose he is making a fool of himself, is he the sort of fellow to stop because one tells him so? I should say not, from what I know of him, and of you."

"I don't know," argued Catherine, looking pleased with her compliment. "You used to have quite an influence over him, if you remember."

"That's quite possible; but then he was a small boy, now he is a grown man."

"But you are a much older one."

"Too old to trust to that."

"And you have been wounded in the war."

"The hotel may be full of wounded officers; if not I might get a little unworthy purchase there. In any case I'll go. I should have to go somewhere before many days. It may as well be to that place as to another. I have heard that the air is glorious; and I'll keep an eye on Robin, if I can't do anything else."

"That's enough for me," cried Catherine, warmly. "I have sufficient faith in you to leave all the rest to your own discretion and good sense and better heart. And I never shall forget it, Duncan, never, never! You are the one person he wouldn't instantly suspect as an emissary, besides being the only one I ever—ever trusted well enough to—to take at your word as I have done."

I thought myself that the sentence might have pursued a bolder course without untruth or necessary complications. Perhaps my conceit was on a scale with my acknowledged infirmity where Catherine was concerned. But I did think that there was more than trust in the eyes that now melted into mine; there was liking at least, and gratitude enough to inspire one to win infinitely more. I went so far as to take in mine the hand to which I had dared to aspire in the temerity of my youth; nor shall I pretend for a moment that the old aspirations had not already mounted to their old seat in my brain. On the contrary, I was only wondering whether the honesty of voicing my hopes would nowise counterbalance the caddishness of the sort of stipulation they might imply.

"All I ask," I was saying to myself, "is that you will give me another chance, and take me seriously this time, if I prove myself worthy in the way you want."

But I am glad to think I had not said it when tea came up, and saved a dangerous situation by breaking an insidious spell.

I stayed another hour at least, and there are few in my memory which passed more deliciously at the time. In writing of it now I feel that I have made too little of Catherine Evers, in my anxiety not to make too much, yet am about to leave her to stand or to fall in the reader's opinion by such impression as I have already succeeded in creating in his or her mind. Let me add one word, or two, while yet I may. A baron's daughter (though you might have known Catherine some time without knowing that), she had nevertheless married for mere love as a very young girl, and had been left a widow before the birth of her boy. I never knew her husband, though we were distant kin, nor yet herself during the long years through which she mourned him. Catherine Evers was beginning to recover her interest in the world when first we met; but she never returned to that identical fold of society in which she had been born and bred. It was, of course, despite her own performances, a fold to which the worldly wolf was no stranger; and her trouble had turned a light-hearted little lady into an eager, intellectual, speculative being, with a sort of shame for her former estate, and an undoubted reactionary dislike of dominion and of petty pomp. Of her own high folk one neither saw nor heard a thing; her friends were the powerful preachers of most denominations, and one or two only painted or wrote; for she had been greatly exercised about religion, and somewhat solaced by the arts.

Of her charm for me, a lad with a sneaking regard for the pen, even when I buckled on the sword, I need not be too analytical. No doubt about her kindly interest, in the first instance, in so morbid a curiosity as a subaltern who cared for books and was prepared to extend his gracious patronage to pictures. This subaltern had only too much money, and if the truth be known, only too little honest interest in the career into which he had allowed himself to drift. An early stage of that career brought him up to London, where family pressure drove him on a day to Elm Park Gardens. The rest is easily conceived. Here was a woman, still young, though some years older than oneself; attractive, intellectual, amusing, the soul of sympathy, at once a spiritual influence and the best companion in the world; and for a time, at least, she had taken a perhaps imprudent interest in a lad whom she so greatly interested herself, on so many and various accounts. Must you marvel that the young fool mistook the interest, on both sides, for a more intense feeling, of which he for one had no experience at the time, and that he fell by his mistake at a ridiculously early stage of his career?

It is, I grant, more surprising to find the same young man playing Harry Esmond (at due distance) to the same Lady Castlewood after years in India and a taste of two wars. But Catherine's room was Catherine's room, a very haunt of the higher sirens, charged with noble promptings and forgotten influences and impossible vows. And you will please bear in mind that as yet I am but setting forth, from this rarefied atmosphere, upon my invidious mission.

CHAPTER II

THE THEATRE OF WAR

It is a far cry to Zermatt at the best of times, and that is not the middle of August. The annual rush was at its height, the trains crowded, the heat of them overpowering. I chose to sit up all night in my corner of an ordinary compartment, as a lesser evil than the *wagon-lit* in which you cannot sit up at all. In the morning one was in Switzerland, with a black collar, a rusty chin, and a countenance in keeping with its appointments. It was not as though the night had been beguiled for me by such considerations as are only proper to the devout pilgrim in his lady's service.

On the contrary, and to tell the honest truth, I found it quite impossible to sustain such a serious view of the very special service to which I was foresworn: the more I thought of it, in one sense, the less in another, until my only chance was to go forward with grim humour in the spirit of impersonal curiosity which that attitude induces. In a word, and the cant one which yet happens to express my state of mind to a nicety, I had already "weakened" on the whole business which I had been in such a foolish hurry to undertake, though not for one reactionary moment upon her for whom I had undertaken it. I was still entirely eager to "do her behest in pleasure or in pain"; but this particular enterprise I was beginning to view apart from its inspiration, on its intrinsic demerits, and the more clearly I saw it in its own light, the less pleasure did the prospect afford me.

A young giant, whom I had not seen since his childhood, was merely understood to be carrying on a conspicuous, but in all probability the most innocent, flirtation in a Swiss hotel; and here was I, on mere second-hand hearsay, crossing half Europe to spoil his perfectly legitimate sport! I did not examine my project from the unknown lady's point of view; it made me quite hot enough to consider it from that of my own sex. Yet, the day before yesterday, I had more than acquiesced in the dubious plan. I had even volunteered for its achievement. The train rattled out one long, maddening tune to my own incessant marvellings at my own secret apostasy: the stuffy compartment was not Catherine's sanctum of the quickening memorials and the olden spell. Catherine herself was no longer before me in the vivacious flesh, with her half playful pathos of word and look, her fascinating outward light and shade, her deeper and steadier intellectual glow. Those, I suppose, were the charms which had undone me, first as well as last; but the memory of them was no solace in the train. Nor was I tempted to dream again of ultimate reward. I could see now no further than my immediate part, and a more distasteful mixture of the mean and of the ludicrous I hope never to rehearse again.

One mitigation I might have set against the rest. Dining at the Rag the night before I left, I met a man who knew a man then staying at the Riffel Alp. My man was a sapper with whom I had had a very slight acquaintance out in India, but he happened to be one of those good-natured creatures who never hesitate to bestir themselves or their friends to oblige a mere acquaintance: he asked if I had secured rooms, and on learning that I had not, insisted on telegraphing to his friend to do his best for me. I had not hitherto appreciated the popularity of a resort which I happened only to know by name, nor did I even on getting at Lausanne a telegram to say that a room was duly reserved for me. It was only when I actually arrived, tired out with travel, toward the second evening, and when half of those who had come up with me were sent down again to Zermatt for their pains, that I felt as grateful as I ought to have been from the beginning. Here upon a mere ledge of the High Alps was a hotel with tier upon tier of windows winking in the setting sun. On every hand were dazzling peaks piled against a turquoise sky, yet drawn respectfully apart from the incomparable Matterhorn, that proud grim chieftain of them all. The grand spectacle and the magic air made me thankful to be there, if only for their sake, albeit the more regretful that a purer purpose had not drawn me to so fine a spot.

My unknown friend at court, one Quinby, a civilian, came up and spoke before I had been five minutes at my destination. He was a very tall and extraordinarily thin man, with an ill-nourished red moustache, and an easy geniality of a somewhat acid sort. He had a trick of laughing softly through his nose, and my two sticks served to excite a sense of humour as odd as its habitual expression.

"I'm glad you carry the outward signs," said he, "for I made the most of your wounds and you really owe your room to them. You see, we're a very representative crowd. That festive old boy, strutting up and down with his cigar, in the Panama hat, is really best known in the black cap: it's old Sankey, the hanging judge. The big man with his back turned you will know in a moment when he looks this way: it's our celebrated friend Belgrave Teale. He comes down in one or other of his parts every day: to-day it's the genial squire, yesterday it was the haw-haw officer of the Crimean school. But a real live officer from the Front we don't happen to have had, much less a wounded one, and you limp straight into the breach."

I should have resented these pleasantries from an ordinary stranger, but this libertine might be held to have earned his charter, and moreover I had further use for him. We were loitering on the steps between the glass veranda and the terrace at the back of the hotel. The little sunlit stage was full of vivid, trivial, transitory life, it seemed as a foil to the vast eternal scene. The hanging judge still strutted with his cigar, peering jocosely from under the broad brim of his Panama; the great actor still posed aloof, the human Matterhorn of the group. I descried no showy woman with a tall youth dancing attendance; among the brick-red English faces there was not one that bore the least resemblance to the latest photograph of Bob Evers.

A little consideration suggested my first move.

"I think I saw a visitors' book in the hall," I said. "I may as well stick down my name."

But before doing so I ran my eye up and down the pages inscribed by those who had arrived that month.

"See anybody you know?" inquired Quinby, who hovered obligingly at my elbow. It was really necessary to be as disingenuous as possible, more especially with a person whose own conversation was evidently quite unguarded.

"Yes, by Jove I do! Robin Evers, of all people!"

"Do you know him?"

The question came pretty quickly. I was sorry I had said so much.

"Well, I once knew a small boy of that name; but then they are not a small clan."

"His mother's the Honourable," said Quinby, with studious unconcern, yet I fancied with increased interest in me.

"I used to see something of them both," I deliberately admitted, "when the lad was little. How has he turned out?"

Quinby gave his peculiar nasal laugh.

"A nice youth," said he. "A very nice youth!"

"Do you mean nice or nasty?" I asked, inclined to bridle at his tone.

"Oh, anything but nasty," said Quinby. "Only—well— perhaps a bit rapid for his years!"

I stooped and put my name in the book before making any further remark. Then I handed Quinby my cigarette-case, and we sat down on the nearest lounge.

"Rapid, is he?" said I. "That's quite interesting. And how does it take him?"

"Oh, not in any way that's discreditable; but as a matter of fact, there's a gay young widow here, and they're fairly going it!"

I lit my cigarette with a certain unexpected sense of downright satisfaction. So there was something in it after all. It had seemed such a fool's errand in the train.

"A young widow," I repeated, emphasising one of Quinby's epithets and ignoring the other.

"I mean, of course, she's a good deal older than Evers."

"And her name?"

"A Mrs. Lascelles."

I nodded.

"Do you happen to know anything about her, Captain Clephane?"

"I can't say I do."

"No more does anybody else," said Quinby, "except that she's an Indian widow of sorts."

"Indian!" I repeated with more interest.

Quinby looked at me.

"You've been out there yourself, perhaps?"

"It was there I knew Hamilton," said I, naming our common friend in the Engineers.

"Yet you're sure you never came across Mrs. Lascelles there?"

"India's a large place," I said, smiling as I shook my head.

"I wonder if Hamilton did," speculated Quinby aloud.

"And the Lascelleses," I added, "are another large clan."

"Well," he went on, after a moment's further cogitation, "there's nobody here can place this particular Mrs. Lascelles;

but there are some who say things which they can tell you themselves. I'm not going to repeat them if you know anything about the boy. I only wish you knew him well enough to give him a friendly word of advice!"

"Is it so bad as all that?"

"My dear sir, I don't say there's anything bad about it," returned Quinby, who seemed to possess a pretty gift of suggestive negation. "But you may hear another opinion from other people, for you will find that the whole hotel is talking about it. No," he went on, watching my eyes, "it's no use looking for them at this time of day; they disappear from morning to night; if you want to see them you must take a stroll when everybody else is thinking of turning in. Then you may have better luck. But here are the letters at last."

The concierge had appeared, hugging an overflowing armful of postal matter. In another minute there was hardly standing room in the little hall. My companion uttered his unlovely laugh.

"And here comes the British lion roaring for his London papers! It isn't his letters he's so keen on, if you notice, Captain Clephane; it's his *Daily Mail*, with the latest cricket, and after that the war. Teale is an exception, of course. He has a stack of press-cuttings every day. You will see him gloating over them in a minute. Ah! the old judge has got his *Sportsman*; he reads nothing else except the *Sporting Times*, and he's going back for the Leger. Do you see the man with the blue spectacles and the peeled nose? He was last Vice Chancellor but one at Cambridge. No, that's not a Bishop, it's an Archdeacon. All we want is a Cabinet Minister now; every evening there is a rumour that the Colonial Secretary is on his way, and most mornings you will hear that he has actually arrived under cloud of night."

The facetious Quinby did not confine his more or less caustic commentary to the well-known folk of whom there seemed no dearth; in the ten or twenty minutes that we sat together he further revealed himself as a copious gossip, with a wide net alike for the big fish and for the smallest fry. There was a sheepish gentleman with a twitching face, and a shaven cleric in close attendance; the former a rich brand plucked from burning by the latter, whose temporal reward was the present trip, so Quinby assured me during the time it took them to pass before our eyes through the now emptying hall. A delightfully boyish young American came inquiring waggishly for his "best girl"; next moment I was given to understand that he meant his bride, who was ten times too good for him, with further trivialities to which the dressing-bell put a timely period. There was no sign of my Etonian when I went upstairs.

As I dressed in my small low room, with its sloping ceiling of varnished wood, at the top of the house, I felt that after all I had learnt nothing really new respecting that disturbing young gentleman. Quinby had already proved himself such an arrant gossip as to discount every word that he had said before I placed him in his proper type: it is one which I have encountered elsewhere, that of the middle-aged bachelor who will and must talk, and he had confessed his celibacy almost in his first breath; but a more pronounced specimen of the type I am in no hurry to meet again. If, however, there was some comfort in the thought of his more than probable exaggerations, there was none at all in the knowledge that these would be, if they had not already been, poured into every tolerant ear in the place, if anything more freely than into mine.

I was somewhat late for dinner, but the scandalous couple were later still, and all the evening I saw nothing of them. That, however, was greatly due to this fellow Quinby, whose

E. W. Hornung

determined offices one could hardly disdain after once accepting favours from him. In the press after dinner I saw his ferret's face peering this way and that, a good head higher than any other, and the moment our eyes met he began elbowing his way toward me. Only an ingrate would have turned and fled; and for the next hour or two I suffered Quinby to exploit my wounds and me for a good deal more than our intrinsic value. To do the man justice, however, I had no fault to find with the very pleasant little circle into which he insisted on ushering me, at one end of the glazed veranda, and should have enjoyed my evening but for an inquisitive anxiety to get in touch with the unsuspecting pair. Meanwhile the lilt of a waltz had mingled with the click of billiard balls and the talking and laughing which make a summer's night vocal in that outpost of pleasure on the silent heights; and some of our party had gone off to dance. In the end I followed them, sticks and all; but there was no Bob Evers among the dancers, nor in the billiard-room, nor anywhere else indoors.

Then, last of all, I looked where Quinby had advised me to look, and there sure enough, on the almost deserted terrace, were the couple whom I had come several hundred miles to put asunder. Hitherto I had only realised the distasteful character of my task; now at a glance I had my first inkling of its difficulty; and there ended the premature satisfaction with which I had learnt that there was "something in" the rumour which had reached Catherine's ears.

There was no moon, but the mountain stars were the brightest I have ever seen in Europe. The mountains themselves stood back, as it were, darkling and unobtrusive; all that was left of the Matterhorn was a towering gap in the stars; and in the faint cold light stood my friends, somewhat close together, and I thought I saw the red tips of two cigarettes. There was at least no mistaking the long loose limbs in the light overcoat. And because a woman always looks relatively taller than a man, this woman looked nearly as tall as this lad.

"Bob Evers? You may not remember me, but my name's Clephane—Duncan, you know!"

I felt the veriest scoundrel, and yet the words came out as smoothly as I have written them, as if to show me that I had been a potential scoundrel all my life.

"Duncan Clephane? Why, of course I remember you. I should think I did! I say, though, you must have had a shocking time!"

Bob's voice was quite quiet for all his astonishment, his manner a miracle, though it was too dark to read the face; and his right hand held tenderly to mine, as his eyes fell upon my sticks, while his left poised a steady cigarette. And now I saw that there was only one red tip after all.

"I read your name in the visitors' book," said I, feeling too big a brute to acknowledge the boy's solicitude for me. "I—I felt certain it must be you."

"How splendid!" cried the great fellow in his easy, soft, unconscious voice, "By the way, may I introduce you to Mrs. Lascelles? Captain Clephane's one of our very oldest friends, just back from the Front, and precious nearly blown to bits!"

E. W. Hornung

CHAPTER III

FIRST BLOOD

Mrs. Lascelles and I exchanged our bows. For a dangerous woman there was a rather striking want of study in her attire. Over the garment which I believe is called a "rain-coat," the night being chilly, she had put on her golf-cape as well, and the effect was a little heterogeneous. It also argued qualities other than those for which I was naturally on the watch. Of the lady's face I could see even less than of Bob's, for the hood of the cape was upturned into a cowl, and even in Switzerland the stars are only stars. But while I peered she let me hear her voice, and a very rich one it was—almost deep in tone—the voice of a woman who would sing contralto.

"Have you really been fighting?" she asked, in a way that was either put on, or else the expression of a more understanding sympathy than one usually provoked; for pity and admiration, and even a helpless woman's envy, might all have been discovered by an ear less critical and more charitable than mine.

"Like anything!" answered Bob, in his unaffected speech.

"Until they knocked me out," I felt bound to add, "and that, unfortunately, was before very long."

"You must have been dreadfully wounded!" said Mrs. Lascelles, raising her eyes from my sticks and gazing at me, I fancied, with some intentness; but at her expression I could only guess.

"Bowled over on Spion Kop," said Bob, "and fairly riddled as he lay."

"But only about the legs, Mrs. Lascelles," I explained; "and you see I didn't lose either, so I've no cause to complain. I had hardly a graze higher up."

"Were you up there the whole of that awful day?" asked Mrs. Lascelles, on a low but thrilling note.

"I'd got to be," said I, trying to lighten the subject with a laugh. But Bob's tone was little better.

"So he went staggering about among his men," he must needs chime in, with other superfluities, "for I remember reading all about it in the papers, and boasting like anything about having known you, Duncan, but feeling simply sick with envy all the time. I say, you'll be a tremendous hero up here, you know! I'm awfully glad you've come. It's quite funny, all the same. I suppose you came to get bucked up? He couldn't have gone to a better place, could he, Mrs. Lascelles?"

"Indeed he could not. I only wish we could empty the hotel and fill every bed with our poor wounded!"

I do not know why I should have felt so much surprised. I had made unto myself my own image of Mrs. Lascelles, and neither her appearance, nor a single word that had fallen from her, was in the least in keeping with my conception. Prepared for a certain type of woman, I was quite confounded by its unconventional embodiment, and inclined to believe that this was not the type at all. I ought to have known life better. The most scheming mind may well entertain an enthusiasm for arms, genuine enough in itself, at a martial crisis, and a natural manner is by no means incompatible with the cardinal vices. That manner and that enthusiasm were absolutely all that I as yet knew in favour of this Mrs. Lascelles; but they were enough to cause me irritation. I wished to be honest with somebody; let me at least be honestly inimical to her. I took out my cigarette-case, and when about to help myself, handed it, with a vile pretence at impulse, to Mrs. Lascelles instead.

Mrs. Lascelles thanked me, in a higher key, but declined.

"Don't you smoke?" I asked blandly.

"Sometimes."

"Ah! then I wasn't mistaken. I thought I saw two cigarettes just now."

Indeed, I had first smelt and afterward discovered the second cigarette smouldering on the ground. Bob was smoking his still. The chances were that they had both been lighted at the same time; therefore the other had been thrown away unfinished at my approach. And that was one more variation from the type of my confident preconceptions.

Young Robin had meanwhile had a quick eye on us both, and the stump of his own cigarette was glowing between a firmer pair of lips than I had looked for in that boyish face.

"It's so funny," said he (but there was no fun in his voice), "the prejudice some people have against ladies smoking. Why shouldn't they? Where's the harm?"

Now there is no new plea to be advanced on either side of this eternal question, nor is it one upon which I ever felt strongly, but just then I felt tempted to speak as though I did. I will not now dissect my motive, but it was vaguely connected with my mission, and not unrighteous from that standpoint. I said it was not a question of harm at all, but of what one admired in a woman, and what one did not: a man loved to look upon a woman as something above and beyond him, and there could be no doubt that the gap seemed a little less when both were smoking like twin funnels. That, I thought, was the adverse point of view; I did not say that it was mine.

"I'm glad to hear it," said Bob Evers, with the faintest coldness in his tone, though I fancied he was fuming within, and admired both his chivalry and his self-control. "To me it's quite funny. I call it sheer selfishness. We enjoy a cigarette ourselves; why shouldn't they? We don't force them to be teetotal, do we? Is it bad form for a lady to drink a glass of wine? You mightn't bicycle once, might you, Mrs. Lascelles? I daresay Captain Clephane doesn't approve of that yet!"

"That's hitting below the belt," said I, laughing. "I wasn't giving you my opinion, but only the old-fashioned view of the matter. I wish you'd take one, Mrs. Lascelles, or I shall think I've been misunderstood all round!"

"No, thank you, Captain Clephane. That old-fashioned feeling is infectious."

"Then I will," cried Bob, "to show there's no ill-feeling. You old fire-eater, I believe you just put up the argument to change the conversation. Wouldn't you like a chair for those game legs?"

"No, I've got to use them in moderation. I was going to have a stroll when I spotted you at last."

"Then we'll all take one together," cried the genial old Bob once more. "It's a bit cold standing here, don't you think, Mrs. Lascelles? After you with the match!"

But I held it so long that he had to strike another, for I had looked on Mrs. Lascelles at last. It was not an obviously interesting face, like Catherine's, but interest there was of another kind. There was nothing intellectual in the low brow, no enthusiasm for books and pictures in the bold eyes, no witticism waiting on the full lips; but in the curve of those lips and the look from those eyes, as in the deep chin and the carriage of the hooded head, there was something perhaps not lower than intellect in the scale of personal equipment. There was, at all events, character and to spare. Even by the brief glimmer of a single match I could see that (and more) for myself. Then came a moment's interval before Bob struck his light, and in that moment her face changed. As I saw it next, it appealed, it entreated, until the second match was flung away. And the appeal was to such purpose that I do not think I was five seconds silent.

"And what do you do with yourself up here all day? I mean you hale people; of course, I can only potter in the sun."

The question, perhaps, was better in intention than in tact. I did not mean them to take it to themselves, but Bob's answer showed that it was open to misconstruction.

"Some people climb," said he; "you'll know them by their noses. The glaciers are almost as bad, though, aren't they,

Mrs. Lascelles? Lots of people potter about the glaciers. It's rather sport in the serracs; you've got to rope. But you'll find lots more loafing about the place all day, reading Tauchnitz novels, and watching people on the Matterhorn through the telescope. That's the sort of thing, isn't it, Mrs. Lascelles?"

She also had misunderstood the drift of my unlucky question. But there was nothing disingenuous in her reply. It reminded me of her eyes, as I had seen them by the light of the first match.

"Mr. Evers doesn't say that he is a climber himself, Captain Clephane; but he is a very keen one, and so am I. We are both beginners, so we have begun together. It's such fun. We do some little thing every day; to-day we did the Schwarzee. You won't be any wiser, and the real climbers wouldn't call it climbing, but it means three thousand feet first and last. To-morrow we are going to the Monte Rosa hut. There is no saying where we shall end up, if this weather holds."

In this fashion Mrs. Lascelles not only made me a contemptuous present of information which I had never sought, but tacitly rebuked poor Bob for his gratuitous attempt at concealment. Clearly, they had nothing to conceal; and the hotel talk was neither more nor less than hotel talk. There was, nevertheless, a certain self-consciousness in the attitude of either (unless I grossly misread them both) which of itself afforded some excuse for the gossips in my own mind.

Yet I did not know; every moment gave me a new point of view. On my remarking, genuinely enough, that I only wished I could go with them, Bob Evers echoed the wish so heartily that I could not but believe that he meant what he said. On his side, in that case, there could be absolutely nothing. And yet, again, when Mrs. Lascelles had left us, as she did ere long in the easiest and most natural manner, and when we had started a last cigarette together, then once more I was not so sure of him.

"That's rather a handsome woman," said I, with perhaps more than the authority to which my years entitled me. But I fancied it would "draw" poor Bob. And it did.

"Rather handsome!" said he, with a soft little laugh not altogether complimentary to me. "Yes, I should almost go as far myself. Still I don't see how *you* know; you haven't so much as seen her, my dear fellow."

"Haven't we been walking up and down outside this lighted veranda for the last ten minutes?"

Bob emitted a pitying puff. "Wait till you see her in the sunlight! There's not many of them can stand it, as they get it up here. But she can—like anything!"

"She has made an impression on you, Bob," said I, but in so sedulously inoffensive a manner that his self-betrayal was all the greater when he told me quite hotly not to be an ass.

Now I was more than ten years his senior, and Bob's manners were as charming as only the manners of a nice Eton boy can be; therefore I held my peace, but with difficulty refrained from nodding sapiently to myself. We took a couple of steps in silence, then Bob stopped short. I did the same. He was still a little stern; we were just within range of the veranda lights, and I can see and hear him to this day, almost as clearly as I did that night.

"I'm not much good at making apologies," he began, with rather less grace than becomes an apologist; but it was more than enough for me from Bob.

"Nor I at receiving them, my dear Bob."

"Well, you've got to receive one now, whether you accept it or not. I was the ass myself, and I beg your pardon!"

Somehow I felt it was a good deal for a lad to say, at that age, and with Bob's upbringing and popularity, even though he said it rather scornfully in the fewest words. The scorn was really for himself, and I could well understand it. Nay, I was glad to have something to forgive in the beginning, I with my unforgivable mission, and would have laughed the matter off without another word if Bob had let me.

"I'm a bit raw on the point," said he, taking my arm for a last turn, "and that's the truth. There was a fellow who came out with me, quite a good chap really, and a tremendous pal of mine at Eton, yet he behaved like a lunatic about this very thing. Poor chap, he reads like anything, and I suppose he'd been overdoing it, for he actually asked me to choose between Mrs. Lascelles and himself! What could a fellow do but let the poor old simpleton go? They seem to think you can't be pals with a woman without wanting to make love to her. Such utter rot! I confess I lose my hair with them; but that doesn't excuse me in the least for losing it with you."

I assured him, on the other hand, that his very natural irritability on the subject made all the difference in the world. "But whom," I added, "do you mean by 'them'? Not anybody else in the hotel?"

"Good heavens, no!" cried Bob, finding a fair target for his scorn at last. "Do you think I care twopence what's said or thought by people I never saw in my life before and am never likely to see again? I know how I'm behaving. What does it matter what they think? Not that they're likely to bother their heads about us any more than we do about them."

E. W. Hornung

"You don't know that."

"I certainly don't care," declared my lordly youth, with obvious sincerity. "No, I was only thinking of poor old George Kennerley and people like him, if there are any. I did care what he thought, that is until I saw he was as mad as anything on the subject. It was too silly. I tell you what, though, I'd value your opinion!" And he came to another stop and confronted me again, but this time such a picture of boyish impulse and of innocent trust in me (even by that faint light) that I was myself strongly inclined to be honest with him on the spot. But I only smiled and shook my head.

"Oh, no, you wouldn't," I assured him.

"But I tell you I would!" he cried. "Do *you* think there's any harm in my going about with Mrs. Lascelles because I rather like her and she rather likes me? I won't condescend to give you my word that I mean none."

What answer could I give? His charming frankness quite disarmed me, and the more completely because I felt that a dignified reticence would have been yet more characteristic of this clean, sweet youth, with his noble unconsciousness alike of evil and of evil speaking. I told him the truth—that there could be no harm at all with such a fellow as himself. And he wrung my hand until he hurt it; but the physical pain was a relief.

Never can I remember going up to bed with a better opinion of another person, or a worse one of myself. How could I go on with my thrice detestable undertaking? Now that I was so sure of him, why should I even think of it for another moment? Why not go back to London and tell his mother that her early confidence had not been misplaced, that the lad did know how to take care of himself, and better still of any woman whom he chose to honour with his bright, pure-hearted friendship? All this I felt as strongly as any conviction I have ever held. Why, then, could I not write it at once to Catherine in as many words?

Strange how one forgets, how I had forgotten in half an hour! The reason came home to me on the stairs, and for the second time.

It had come home first by the light of those two matches, struck outside in the dark part of the deserted terrace. It was not the lad whom I distrusted, but the woman of whose face I had then obtained my only glimpse—that night.

I had known her, after all, in India years before.

CHAPTER IV

A LITTLE KNOWLEDGE

Once in the Town Hall at Simla (the only time I was ever there) it was my fortune to dance with a Mrs. Heymann of Lahore, a tall woman, but a featherweight partner, and in all my dancing days I never had a better waltz. To my delight she had one other left, though near the end, and we were actually dancing when an excitable person came out of the card-room, flushed with liquor and losses, and carried her off in the most preposterous manner. It was a shock to me at the time to learn that this outrageous little man was my partner's husband. Months later, when I came across their case in the papers, it was, I am afraid, without much sympathy for the injured husband. The man was quite unpresentable, and I had seen no more of him at Simla, but of the woman just enough to know her by matchlight on the terrace at the Riffel Alp.

And this was Bob's widow, this dashing *divorcee*! Dashing she was as I now remembered her, fine in mould, finer in spirit, reckless and rebellious as she well might be. I had seen her submit before a ball-room, but with the contempt that leads captivity captive. Seldom have I admired anything more. It was splendid even to remember, the ready outward obedience, the not less apparent indifference and disdain. There was a woman whom any man might admire, who had

had it in her to be all things to some man! But Bob Evers was not a man at all. And this—and this—was his widow!

Was she one at all? How could I tell? Yes, it was Lascelles, the other name in the case, to the best of my recollection. But had she any right to bear it? And even supposing they had married, what had happened to the second husband? Widow or no widow, second marriage or no second marriage, defensible or indefensible, was this the right friend for a lad still fresh from Eton, the only son of his mother, who had sent me in secret to his side?

There was only one answer to the last question, whatever might be said or urged in reply to all the rest. I could not but feel that Catherine Evers had been justified in her instinct to an almost miraculous degree; that her worst fears were true enough, so far as the lady was concerned; and that Providence alone could have inspired her to call in an agent who knew what I knew, and who therefore saw his duty as plainly as I already saw mine. But it is one thing to recognise a painful duty and quite another thing to know how to minimise the pain to those most affected by its performance. The problem was no easy one to my mind, and I lay awake upon it far into the night.

Tired out with travel, I fell asleep in the end, to awake with a start in broad daylight. The sun was pouring through the uncurtained dormer-window of my room under the roof. And in the sunlight, looking his best in knickerbockers, as only thin men do, with face greased against wind and glare, and blue spectacles in rest upon an Alpine wideawake, stood the lad who had taken his share in keeping me awake.

"I'm awfully sorry," he began. "It's horrid cheek, but when I saw your room full of light I thought you might have been even earlier than I was. You must get them to give you curtains up here."

He had a note in his hand and I thought by his manner there was something that he wished and yet hesitated to tell me. I accordingly asked him what it was.

"It's what we were speaking about last night!" burst out Bob. "That's why I've come to you. It's these silly fools who can't mind their own business and think everybody else is like themselves! Here's a note from Mrs. Lascelles which makes it plain that that old idiot George is not the only one who has been talking about us, and some of the talk has reached her ears. She doesn't say so in so many words, but I can see it's that. She wants to get out of our expedition to Monte Rosa hut—wants me to go alone. The question is, ought I to let her get out of it? Does it matter one rap what this rabble says about us? I've come to ask your advice—you were such a brick about it all last night—and what you say I'll do."

I had begun to smile at Bob's notion of "a rabble": this one happened to include a few quite eminent men, as you have seen, to say nothing of the average quality of the crowd, of which I had been able to form some opinion of my own. But I had already noticed in Bob the exclusiveness of the type to which he belonged, and had welcomed it as one does welcome the little faults of the well-night faultless. It was his last sentence that made me feel too great a hypocrite to go on smiling.

"It may not matter to you," I said at length, "but it may to the lady."

"I suppose it does matter more to them?"

The sunburnt face, puckered with a wry wistfulness, was only comic in its incongruous coat of grease. But I was under no temptation to smile. I had to confine my mind pretty closely to the general principle, and rather studiously to ignore the particular instance, before I could bring myself to answer the almost infantile inquiry in those honest eyes.

"My dear fellow, it must!"

Bob looked disappointed but resigned.

"Well, then, I won't press it, though I'm not sure that I agree. You see, it's not as though there was or ever would be anything between us. The idea's absurd. We are absolute pals and nothing else. That's what makes all this such a silly bore. It's so unnecessary. Now she wants me to go alone, but I don't see the fun of that."

"Does she ask you to go alone?"

"She does. That's the worst of it."

I nodded, and he asked me why.

"She probably thinks it would be the best answer to the tittle-tattlers, Bob."

That was not a deliberate lie; not until the words were out did it occur to me that Mrs. Lascelles might now have another object in getting rid of her swain for the day. But Bob's eyes lighted in a way that made me feel a deliberate liar.

"By Jove!" he said, "I never thought of that. I don't agree with her, mind, but if that's her game I'll play it like a book. So long, Duncan! I'm not one of those chaps who ask a man's advice without the slightest intention of ever taking it!"

"But I haven't ventured to advise you," I reminded the boy, with a cowardly eye to the remotest consequences.

"Perhaps not, but you've shown me what's the proper thing to do." And he went away to do it there and then, like the blameless exception that I found him to so many human rules.

I had my breakfast upstairs after this, and lay for some considerable time a prey to feelings which I shall make no further effort to expound; for this interview had not altered, but only intensified them; and in any case they must be obvious to those who take the trouble to conceive themselves in my unenviable position.

And it was my ironic luck to be so circumstanced in a place where I could have enjoyed life to the hilt! Only to lie with the window open was to breathe air of a keener purity, a finer temper, a more exhilarating freshness, than had ever before entered my lungs; and to get up and look out of the window was to peer into the limpid brilliance of a gigantic crystal, where the smallest object was in startling focus, and the very sunbeams cut with scissors. The people below trailed shadows like running ink. The light was ultra-tropical. One looked for drill suits and pith headgear, and was amazed to find pajamas insufficient at the open window.

Upon the terrace on the other side, when I eventually came down, there were cane chairs and Tauchnitz novels under the umbrella tents, and the telescope out and trained upon a party on the Matterhorn. A group of people were waiting turns at the telescope, my friend Quinby and the hanging judge among them. But I searched under the umbrella tents as well as one could from the top of the steps before hobbling down to join the group.

"I have looked for an accident through that telescope," said the jocose judge, "fifteen Augusts running. They usually have one the day after I go."

"Good morning, sir!" was Quinby's greeting; and I was instantly introduced to Sir John Sankey, with such a parade of my military history as made me wince and Sir John's eye twinkle. I fancied he had formed an unkind estimate of my rather overpowering friend, and lived to hear my impression confirmed in unjudicial language. But our first conversation was about the war, and it lasted until the judge's turn came for the telescope.

"Black with people!" he ejaculated. "They ought to have a constable up there to regulate the traffic."

But when I looked it was long enough before my inexperienced eye could discern the three midges strung on the single strand of cobweb against the sloping snow.

"They are coming down," explained the obliging Quinby. "That's one of the most difficult places, the lower edge of the top slope. It's just a little way along to the right where the first accident was.... By the way, your friend Evers says he's going to do the Matterhorn before he goes."

It was unwelcome hearing, for Quinby had paused to regale me with a lightning sketch of the first accident, and no one had contradicted his gruesome details.

"*Is* young Evers a friend of yours?" inquired the judge.

"He is."

The judge did not say another word. But Quinby availed himself of the first opportunity of playing Ancient Mariner to

E. W. Hornung

my Wedding Guest.

"I saw you talking to them," he told me confidentially, "last night, you know!"

"Indeed."

He took me by the sleeve.

"Of course I don't know what you said, but it's evidently had an effect. Evers has gone off alone for the first time since he has been here."

I shifted my position.

"You evidently keep an eye on him, Mr. Quinby."

"I do, Clephane. I find him a diverting study. He is not the only one in this hotel. There's old Teale on his balcony at the present minute, if you look up. He has the best room in the hotel; the only trouble is that it doesn't face the sun all day; he's not used to being in the shade, and you'll hear him damn the limelight-man in heaps one of these fine mornings. But your enterprising young friend is a more amusing person than Belgrave Teale."

I had heard enough of my enterprising young friend from this quarter.

"Do you never make any expeditions yourself, Mr. Quinby?"

"Sometimes." Quinby looked puzzled. "Why do you ask?" he was constrained to add.

"You should have volunteered instead of Mrs. Lascelles to-day. It would have been an excellent opportunity for prosecuting your own rather enterprising studies."

One would have thought that one's displeasure was plain enough at last; but not a bit of it. So far from resenting the rebuff, the fellow plucked my sleeve, and I saw at a glance that he had not even listened to my too elaborate sarcasm.

"Talk of the—lady!" he whispered. "Here she comes."

And a second glance intercepted Mrs. Lascelles on the steps, with her bold good looks and her fine upstanding carriage, cut clean as a diamond in that intensifying atmosphere, and hardly less dazzling to the eye. Yet her cotton gown was simplicity's self; it was the right setting for such natural brilliance, a brilliance of eyes and teeth and colouring, a more uncommon brilliance of expression. Indeed it was a wonderful expression, brave rather than sweet, yet capable of sweetness too, and for the moment at least nobly free from the defensive bitterness which was to mark it later. So she stood upon the steps, the talk of the hotel, trailing, with characteristic independence, a cane chair behind her, while she sought a shady place for it, even as I had stood seeking for her: before she found one I was hobbling toward her.

"Oh, thanks, Captain Clephane, but I couldn't think of allowing you! Well, then, between us, if you insist. Here under the wall, I think, is as good a place as any."

She pointed out a clear space in the rapidly narrowing ribbon of shade, and there I soon saw Mrs. Lascelles settled with her book (a trashy novel, that somehow brought Catherine Evers rather sharply before my mind's eye) in an isolation as complete as could be found upon the crowded terrace, and too intentional on her part to permit of an intrusion on mine. I lingered a moment, nevertheless.

E. W. Hornung

"So you didn't go to that hut after all, Mrs. Lascelles?"

"No." She waited a moment before looking up at me. "And I'm afraid Mr. Evers will never forgive me," she added after her look, in the rich undertone that had impressed me overnight, before the cigarette controversy.

I was not going to say that I had seen Bob before he started, but it was an opportunity of speaking generally of the lad. Thus I found myself commenting on the coincidence of our meeting again—he and I—and again lying before I realised that it was a lie. But Mrs. Lascelles sat looking up at me with her fine and candid eyes, as though she knew as well as I which was the real coincidence, and knew that I knew into the bargain. It gave me the disconcerting sensation of being detected and convicted at one blow. Bob Evers failed me as a topic, and I stood like the fool I felt.

"I am sure you ought not to stand about so much, Captain Clephane."

Mrs. Lascelles was smiling faintly as I prepared to take her hint.

"Doesn't it really do you any harm?" she inquired in time to detain me.

"No, just the opposite. I am ordered to take all the exercise I can."

"Even walking?"

"Even hobbling, Mrs. Lascelles, if I don't overdo it."

She sat some moments in thought. I guessed what she was thinking, and I was right.

"There are some lovely walks quite near, Captain Clephane. But you have to climb a little, either going or coming."

"I could climb a little," said I, making up my mind. "It's within the meaning of the act—it would do me good. Which way will you take me, Mrs. Lascelles?"

Mrs. Lascelles looked up quickly, surprised at a boldness on which I was already complimenting myself. But it is the only way with a bold woman.

"Did I say I would take you at all, Captain Clephane?"

"No, but I very much hope you will."

And our eyes met as fairly as they had done by matchlight the night before.

"Then I will," said Mrs. Lascelles, "because I want to speak to you."

CHAPTER V

A MARKED WOMAN

We had come farther than was wise without a rest, but all the seats on the way were in full view of the hotel, and I had been irritated by divers looks and whisperings as we traversed the always crowded terrace. Bob Evers, no doubt, would have turned a deaf ear and a blind eye to them. I myself could pretend to do so, but pretence was evidently one of my strong points. I had not Bob's fine natural regardlessness, for all my seniority and presumably superior knowledge of the world.

So we had climbed the zigzags to the right of the Riffelberg and followed the footpath overlooking the glacier, in the silence enjoined by single file, but at last we were seated on the hillside, a trifle beyond that emerald patch which some humourist has christened the Cricket-ground. Beneath us were the serracs of the Gorner Glacier, teased and tousled like a fringe of frozen breakers. Beyond the serracs was the main stream of comparatively smooth ice, with its mourning band of moraine, and beyond that the mammoth sweep and curve of the Theodule where these glaciers join. Peak after peak of dazzling snow dwindled away to the left. Only the gaunt Riffelhorn reared a brown head against the blue. And there we sat, Mrs. Lascelles and I, with all this before us and a rock behind, while I wondered what my companion meant to say, and how she would begin.

I had not to wonder long.

"You were very good to me last night, Captain Clephane."

There was evidently no beating about the bush for Mrs. Lascelles. I thoroughly approved, but was nevertheless somewhat embarrassed for the moment.

"I—really I don't know how, Mrs. Lascelles!"

"Oh, yes, you do, Captain Clephane; you recognised me at a glance, as I did you."

"I certainly thought I did," said I, poking about with the ferrule of one of my sticks.

"You know you did."

"You are making me know it."

"Captain Clephane, you knew it all along; but we won't argue that point. I am not going to deny my identity. It is very good of you to give me the chance, if rather unnecessary. I am not a criminal. Still you could have made me feel like one, last night, and heaps of men would have done so, either for the fun of it or from want of tact."

I looked inquiringly at Mrs. Lascelles. She could tell me what she pleased, but I was not going to anticipate her by displaying an independent knowledge of matters which she might still care to keep to herself. If she chose to open up a painful subject, well, the pain be upon her own head. Yet I must say that there was very little of it in her face as our eyes met. There was the eager candour that one could not help admiring, with the glowing look of gratitude which I had done so ridiculously little to earn; but the fine flushed face betrayed neither pain, nor shame, nor the affectation of one or the other. There was a certain shyness with the candour. That was all.

"You know quite well what I mean," continued Mrs. Lascelles, with a genuine smile at my disingenuous face. "When you met me before it was under another name, which you have probably quite forgotten."

"No, I remember it."

"Do you remember my husband?"

"Perfectly."

"Did you ever hear—"

Her lip trembled. I dropped my eyes.

"Yes," I admitted, "or rather I saw it for myself in the papers. It's no use pretending I didn't, nor yet that I was the least bit surprised or—or anything else!"

That was not one of my tactful speeches. It was culpably, might indeed have been wilfully, ambiguous; and yet it was the kind of clumsy and impulsive utterance which has the ring of a good intention, and is thus inoffensive except to such as seek excuses for offence. My instincts about Mrs. Lascelles did not place her in this category at all. Nevertheless, the ensuing pause was long enough to make me feel uneasy, and my companion only broke it as I was in the act of framing an apology.

"May I bore you, Captain Clephane?" she asked abruptly. I looked at her once more. She had regained an equal mastery of face and voice, and the admirable candour of her eyes was undimmed by the smallest trace of tears.

"You may try," said I, smiling with the obvious gallantry.

"If I tell you something about myself from that time on, will you believe what I say?"

"You are the last person whom I should think of disbelieving."

"Thank you, Captain Clephane."

"On the other hand, I would much rather you didn't say anything that gave you pain, or that you might afterward regret."

There was a touch of weariness in Mrs. Lascelles's smile, a rather pathetic touch to my mind, as she shook her head.

"I am not very sensitive to pain," she remarked. "That is the one thing to be said for having to bear a good deal while you are fairly young. I want you to know more about me, because I believe you are the only person here who knows anything at all. And then—you didn't give me away last night!"

I pointed to the grassy ledge in front of us, such a vivid green against the house now a hundred feet below.

"I am not pushing you over there," I said. "I take about as much credit for that."

"Ah," sighed Mrs. Lascelles, "but that dear boy, who turns out to be a friend of yours, he knows less than anybody else! He doesn't even suspect. It would have hurt me, yes, it would have hurt even me, to be given away to him! You didn't do it while I was there, and I know you didn't when I had turned my back."

"Of course you know I didn't," I echoed rather testily as I took out a cigarette. The case reminded me of the night before. But I did not again hand it to Mrs. Lascelles.

"Well, then," she continued, "since you didn't give me away, even without thinking, I want you to know that after all there isn't quite so much to give away as there might have been. A divorce, of course, is always a divorce; there is no getting away from that, or from mine. But I really did marry again. And I really am the widow they think I am."

I looked quickly up at her, in pure pity and compassion for one gone so far in sorrow and yet such a little way in life. It was a sudden feeling, an unpremeditated look, but I might as well have spoken aloud. Mrs. Lascelles read me unerringly, and she shook her head, sadly but decidedly, while her eyes gazed calmly into mine.

"*It* was not a happy marriage, either," she said, as impersonally as if speaking of another woman. "You may think what you like of me for saying so to a comparative stranger; but I won't have your sympathy on false pretences, simply because Major Lascelles is dead. Did you ever meet him, by the way?"

And she mentioned an Indian regiment. But the major and I had never met.

"Well, it was not very happy for either of us. I suppose such marriages never are. I know they are never supposed to be. Even if the couple are everything to each other, there is all the world to point his finger, and all the world's wife to turn her back, and you have to care a good deal to get over that. But you may have been desperate in the first instance; you may have said to yourself that the fire couldn't be much worse than the frying-pan. In that case, of course, you deserve no sympathy, and nothing is more irritating to me than the sympathy I don't deserve. It's a matter of temperament; I'm obliged to speak out, even if it puts people more against me than they were already. No, you needn't say anything, Captain Clephane; you didn't express your sympathy, I stopped you in time.... And yet it is rather hard, when one's still reasonably young, with almost everything before one—to be a marked woman all one's time!"

Up to her last words, despite an inviting pause after almost every sentence, I had succeeded in holding my tongue; though she was looking wistfully now at the distant snow-peaks and obviously bestowing upon herself the sympathy she did not want from me (as I had been told in so many words, if not more plainly in the accompanying brief encounter between our eyes), yet had I resisted every temptation to put in my word, until these last two or three from Mrs. Lascelles. They, however, demanded a denial, and I told her it was absurd to describe herself in such terms.

"I am marked," she persisted, "wherever I go I may be known, as you knew me here. If it hadn't been you it would have been somebody else, and I should have known of it indirectly instead of directly; but even supposing I had escaped altogether at this hotel, the next one would probably have made up for it."

"Do you stay much in hotels?"

There had been something in the mellow voice which made such a question only natural, yet it was scarcely asked before I would have given a good deal to recall it.

E. W. Hornung

"There is nowhere else to stay," said Mrs. Lascelles, "unless one sets up house alone, which is costlier and far less comfortable. You see, one does make a friend or two sometimes—before one is found out."

"But surely your people—"

This time I did check myself.

"My people," said Mrs. Lascelles, "have washed their hands of me."

"But Major Lascelles—surely *his* people—"

"They washed their hands of him! You see, they would be the first to tell you, he had always been rather wild; but his crowning act of madness in their eyes was his marriage. It was worse than the worst thing he had ever done before. Still, it is not for me to say anything, or feel anything, against his family...."

And then I knew that they were making her an allowance; it was more than I wanted to know; the ground was too delicate, and led nowhere in particular. Still, it was difficult not to take a certain amount of interest in a handsome woman who had made such a wreck of her life so young, who was so utterly alone, so proud and independent in her loneliness, and apparently quite fine-hearted and unspoilt. But for Bob Evers and his mother, the interest that I took might have been a little different in kind; but even with my solicitude for them there mingled already no small consideration for the social solitary whom I watched now as she sat peering across the glacier, the foremost figure in a world of high lights and great backgrounds, and whom to watch was to admire, even against the greatest of them all. Alas! mere admiration could not change my task or stay my hand; it could but clog me by destroying my singleness of purpose, and giving me a double heart to match my double face.

Since, however, a detestable duty had been undertaken, and since as a duty it was more apparent than I had dreamt of finding it, there was nothing for it but to go through with the thing and make immediate enemies of my friends. So I set my teeth and talked of Bob. I was glad Mrs. Lascelles liked him. His father was a remote connection of mine, whom I had never met. But I had once known his mother very well.

"And what is she like?" asked Mrs. Lascelles, calling her fine eyes home from infinity, and fixing them once more on me.

CHAPTER VI

OUT OF ACTION

Now if, upon a warm, soft, summer evening, you were suddenly asked to describe the perfect winter's day, either you would have to stop and think a little, or your imagination is more elastic than mine. Yet you might have a passionate preference for cold sun and bracing airs. To me, Catherine Evers and this Mrs. Lascelles were as opposite to each other as winter and summer, or the poles, or any other notorious antitheses. There was no comparison between them in my mind, yet as I sat with one among the sunlit, unfamiliar Alps, it was a distinct effort to picture the other in the little London room I knew so well. For it was always among her books and pictures that I thought of Catherine, and to think was to wish myself there at her side, rather than to wish her here at mine. Catherine's appeal, I used to think, was to the highest and the best in me, to brain and soul, and young ambition, and withal to one's love of wit and sense of humour. Mrs. Lascelles, on the other hand, struck me primarily in the light of some splendid and spirited animal. I still liked to dwell upon her dancing. She satisfied the mere eye more and more. But I had no reason to suppose that she knew right from wrong in art or literature, any more than she would seem to have distinguished between them in life itself. Her Tauchnitz novel lay beside her on the grass and I again reflected that it would not have found a place on Catherine's loftiest shelf. Catherine would have raved about the view and made delicious fun of Quinby and the judge, and we should have sat together talking poetry and harmless scandal by the happy hour. Mrs. Lascelles probably took place and people alike for granted. But she had lived, and as an animal she was superb! I looked again into her healthy face and speaking eyes, with their bitter knowledge of good and evil, their scorn of scorn, their redeeming honesty and candour. The contrast was complete in every detail except the widowhood of both women; but I did not pursue it any farther; for once more there was but one woman in my thoughts, and she sat near me under a red parasol—clashing so humanly with the everlasting snows!

"You don't answer my question, Captain Clephane. How much for your thoughts?"

"I'll make you a present of them, Mrs. Lascelles. I was beginning to think that a lot of rot has been written about the eternal snows and the mountain-tops and all the rest of it. There a few lines in that last little volume of Browning—"

I stopped of my own accord, for upon reflection the lines would have made a rather embarrassing quotation. But meanwhile Mrs. Lascelles had taken alarm on other grounds.

"Oh, *don't* quote Browning!"

"Why not?"

"He is far too deep for me; besides, I don't care for poetry, and I was asking you about Mrs. Evers."

"Well," I said, with some little severity, "she's a very clever woman."

"Clever enough to understand Browning?"

"Quite."

If this was irony, it was also self-restraint, for it was to Catherine's enthusiasm that I owed my own. The debt was one of such magnitude as a life of devotion could scarcely have repaid, for to whom do we owe so much as to those who first lifted the scales from our eyes and awakened within us a soul for all such things? Catherine had been to me what I instantly desired to become to this benighted beauty; but the desire was not worth entertaining, since I hardly expected to be many minutes longer on speaking terms with Mrs. Lascelles. I recalled the fact that it was I who had broached the subject of Bob Evers and his mother, together with my unpalatable motive for so doing. And I was seeking in my mind, against the grain, I must confess, for a short cut back to Bob, when Mrs. Lascelles suddenly led the way.

"I don't think," said she, "that Mr. Evers takes after his mother."

"I'm afraid he doesn't," I replied, "in that respect."

"And I am glad," she said. "I do like a boy to be a boy. The only son of his mother is always in danger of becoming something else. Tell me, Captain Clephane, are they very devoted to each other?"

There was some new note in that expressive voice of hers. Was it merely wistful, was it really jealous, or was either element the product of my own imagination? I made answer while I wondered:

"Absolutely devoted, I should say; but it's years since I saw them together. Bob was a small boy then, and one of the jolliest. Still I never expected him to grow up the charming chap he is now."

Mrs. Lascelles sat gazing at the great curve of Theodule Glacier. I watched her face.

"He *is* charming," she said at length. "I am not sure that I ever met anybody quite like him, or rather I am quite sure that I never did. He is so quiet, in a way, and yet so wonderfully confident and at ease!"

"That's Eton," said I. "He is the best type of Eton boy, and the best type of Eton boy," I declared, airing the little condition with a flourish, "is one of the greatest works of God."

"I daresay you're right," said Mrs. Lascelles, smiling indulgently; "but what is it? How do you define it? It isn't 'side,' and yet I can quite imagine people who don't know him thinking that it is. He is cocksure of himself, but of nothing else; that seems to me to be the difference. No one could possibly be more simple in himself. He may have the assurance of a man of fifty, yet it isn't put on; it's neither bumptious nor affected, but just as natural in Mr. Evers as shyness and awkwardness in the ordinary youth one meets. And he has the *savoir faire* not to ask questions!"

Were we all mistaken? Was this the way in which a designing woman would speak of the object of her designs? Not that I thought so hardly of Mrs. Lascelles myself; but I did think that she might well fall in love with Bob Evers, at least as well as he with her. Was this, then, the way in which a woman would be likely to speak of the young man with whom she had fallen in love? To me the appreciation sounded too frank and discerning and acute. Yet I could not

　　　　　E. W. Hornung

call it dispassionate, and frankness was this woman's outstanding merit, though I was beginning to discover others as well. Moreover, the fact remained that they had been greatly talked about; that at any rate must be stopped and I was there to stop it.

I began to pick my words.

"It's all Eton, except what is in the blood, and it's all a question of manners, or rather of manner. Don't misunderstand me, Mrs. Lascelles. I don't say that Bob isn't independent in character as well as in his ways, but only that when all's said he's still a boy and not a man. He can't possibly have a man's experience of the world, or even of himself. He has a young head on his shoulders, after all, if not a younger one than many a boy with half the assurance that you admire in him."

Mrs. Lascelles looked at me point-blank.

"Do you mean that he can't take care of himself?"

"I don't say that."

"Then what do you say?"

The fine eyes met mine without a flicker. The full mouth was curved at the corners in a tolerant, unsuspecting smile. It was hard to have to make an enemy of so handsome and good-humoured a woman. And was it necessary, was it even wise? As I hesitated she turned and glanced downward once more toward the glacier, then rose and went to the lip of our grassy ledge, and as she returned I caught the sound which she had been the first to hear. It was the gritty planting of nailed boots upon a hard, smooth rock.

"I'm afraid you can't say it now," whispered Mrs. Lascelles. "Here's Mr. Evers himself, coming this way back from the Monte Rosa hut! I'm going to give him a surprise!"

And it was a genuine one that she gave him, for I heard his boyish greeting before I saw his hot brown face, and there was no mistaking the sudden delight of both. It was sudden and spontaneous, complete, until his eyes lit on me. Even then his smile did not disappear, but it changed, as did his tone.

"Good heavens!" cried Bob. "How on earth did *you* get up here? By rail to the Riffelberg, I hope?"

"On my sticks."

"It was much too far for him," added Mrs. Lascelles, "and all my fault for showing him the way. But I'm afraid there was contributory obstinacy in Captain Clephane, because he simply wouldn't turn back. And now tell us about yourself, Mr. Evers; surely we were not coming back this way?"

"*We* were not," said Bob, with a something sardonic in his little laugh, "but I thought I might as well. It's the long way, six miles on end upon the glacier."

"But have you really been to the hut?"

"Rather!"

"And where's our guide?"

"Oh, I wouldn't be bothered with a guide all to myself."

"My dear young man, you might have stepped straight into a crevasse!"

E. W. Hornung

"I precious nearly did," laughed Bob, again with something odd about his laughter; "but I say, do you know, if you won't think me awfully rude, I'll push on back and get changed. I'm as hot as anything and not fit to be seen."

And he was gone after very little more than a minute from first to last, gone with rather an elaborate salute to Mrs. Lascelles, and rather a cavalier nod to me. But then neither of us had made any effort to detain him and a notable omission I thought it in Mrs. Lascelles, though to the lad himself it may well have seemed as strange in the old friend as in the new.

"What was it," asked Mrs. Lascelles, when we were on our way home, "that you were going to say about Mr. Evers when he appeared in the flesh in that extraordinary way?"

"I forget," said I, immorally.

"Really? So soon? Don't you remember, I thought you meant that he couldn't take care of himself, and you were just going to tell me what you did mean?"

"Oh, well, it wasn't that, because he can!"

But, as a matter of fact, I had seen my way to taking care of Master Bob without saying a word either to him or to Mrs. Lascelles, or at all events without making enemies of them both.

CHAPTER VII

SECOND FIDDLE

My plan was quite obvious in its simplicity, and not in the least discreditable from my point of view. It was perhaps inevitable that a boy like Bob should imagine I was trying to "cut him out," as my blunt friend Quinby phrased it to my face. I had not, of course, the smallest desire to do any such vulgar thing. All I wanted was to make myself, if possible, as agreeable to Mrs. Lascelles as this youth had done before me, and in any case to share with him all the perils of her society. In other words I meant to squeeze into "the imminent deadly breach" beside Bob Evers, not necessarily in front of him. But if there was nothing dastardly in this, neither was there anything heroic, since I was proof against that kind of deadliness if Bob was not.

On the other hand, the whole character of my mission was affected by the decision at which I had now arrived. There was no longer a necessity to speak plainly to anybody. That odious duty was eliminated from my plan of campaign, and the "frontal attack" of recent history discarded for the "turning movement" of the day. So I had learnt something in South Africa after all. I had learnt how to avoid hard knocks which might very well do more harm than good to the cause I had at heart. That cause was still sharply defined before my

E. W. Hornung

mind. It was the first and most sacred consideration. I wrote a reassuring despatch to Catherine Evers, and took it myself to the little post-office opposite the hotel that very evening before dressing for dinner. But I cannot say that I was thinking of Catherine when I proceeded to spoil three successive ties in the tying.

Yet I can only repeat that I felt absolutely "proof" against the real cause of my solicitude. It is the most delightful feeling where a handsome woman is concerned. The judgment is not warped by passion or clouded by emotion; you see the woman as she is, not as you wish to see her, and if she disappoint it does not matter. You are not left to choose between systematic self-deception and a humiliating admission of your mistake. The lady has not been placed upon an impossible pedestal, and she has not toppled down. In this case the lady started at the most advantageous disadvantage; every admirable quality, her candour, her courage, her spirited independence, her evident determination to piece a broken life together again and make the best of it, told doubly in her favour to me with my special knowledge of her past. It would be too much to say that I was deeply interested; but Mrs. Lascelles had inspired me with a certain sympathy and dispassionate regard. Cultivated she was not, in the conventional sense, but she knew more than can be imbibed from books. She knew life at first hand, had drained the cup for herself, and yet could savour the lees. Not that she enlarged any further on her own past. Mrs. Lascelles was never a great talker, like Catherine; but she was certainly a woman to whom one could talk. And talk to her I did thenceforward, with a conscientious conviction that I was doing my duty, and only an occasional qualm for its congenial character, while Bob listened with a wondering eye, or went his own way without a word.

It is easy to criticise my conduct now. It would have been

difficult to act otherwise at the time. I am speaking of the evening after my walk with Mrs. Lascelles, of the next day when it rained, and now of my third night at the hotel. The sky had cleared. The glass was high. There was a finer edge than ever on the silhouetted mountains against the stars. It appeared that Bob and Mrs. Lascelles had talked of taking their lunch to the Findelen Glacier on the next fine day, for he came up and reminded her of it as she sat with me in the glazed veranda after dinner. I had seen him standing alone under the stars a few minutes before: so this was the result of his cogitation. But in his manner there was nothing studied, much less awkward, and his smile even included me, though he had not spoken to me alone all day.

"Oh, no, I hadn't forgotten, Mr. Evers. I am looking forward to it," said my companion, with a smile of her own to which the most jealous swain could not have taken exception.

Bob Evers looked hard at me.

"You'd better come, too," he said.

"It's probably too far," said I, quite intending to play second fiddle next day, for it was really Bob's turn.

"Not for a man who has been up to the Cricket-ground," he rejoined.

"But it's dreadfully slippery," put in Mrs. Lascelles, with a sympathetic glance at my sticks.

"Let him get them shod like alpenstocks," quoth Bob, "and nails in his boots; then they'll be ready when he does the Matterhorn!"

It might have passed for boyish banter, but I knew that it was something more; the use of the third person changed from chaff to scorn as I listened, and my sympathetic resolution went to the winds.

"Thank you," I replied; "in that case I shall be delighted to come, and I'll take your tip at once by giving orders about my boots."

And with that I resigned my chair to Bob, not sorry for the chance; he should not be able to say that I had monopolised Mrs. Lascelles without intermission from the first. Nevertheless, I was annoyed with him for what he had said, and for the moment my actions were no part of my scheme. Consequently I was thus in the last mood for a familiarity from Quinby, who was hanging about the door between the veranda and the hall, and who would not let me pass.

"That's awfully nice of you," he had the impudence to whisper.

"What do you mean?"

"Giving that poor young beggar another chance!"

"I don't understand you."

"Oh, I like that! You know very well that you've gone in on the military ticket and deliberately cut the poor youngster—"

I did not wait to hear the end of this gratuitous observation. It was very rude of me, but in another minute I should have been guilty of a worse affront. My annoyance had deepened into something like dismay. It was not only Bob Evers who was misconstruing my little attentions to Mrs. Lascelles. I was more or less prepared for that. But here were outsiders talking about us—the three of us! So far from putting a stop to the talk, I had given it a regular fillip: here were Quinby and his friends as keen as possible to see what would happen next, if not betting on a row. The situation had taken a sudden turn for the worse. I forgot the pleasant hours that I had passed with Mrs. Lascelles, and began to wish myself well out of the whole affair. But I had now no intention of getting out of the glacier expedition. I would not have missed it on any account. Bob had brought that on himself.

And I daresay we seemed a sufficiently united trio as we marched along the pretty winding path to the Findelen next morning. Dear Bob was not only such a gentleman, but such a man, that it was almost a pleasure to be at secret issue with him; he would make way for me at our lady's side, listen with interest when she made me spin my martial yarns, laugh if there was aught to laugh at, and in a word, give me every conceivable chance. His manners might have failed him for one heated moment overnight; they were beyond all praise this morning; and I repeatedly discerned a morbid sporting dread of giving the adversary less than fair play. It was sad to me to consider myself as such to Catherine's son, but I was determined not to let the thought depress me, and there was much outward occasion for good cheer. The morning was a perfect one in every way. The rain had released all the pungent aromas of the mountain woods through which we passed. Snowy height came in dazzling contrast with a turquoise sky. The toy town of Zermatt spattered the green hollow far below. And before me on the narrow path went Bob Evers in a flannel suit, followed by Mrs. Lascelles and her red parasol, though he carried her alpenstock with his own in readiness for the glacier.

Thither we came in this order, I at least very hot from hard hobbling to keep up; but the first breath from the glacier cooled me like a bath, and the next like the great drink in the second stanza of the Ode to a Nightingale. I could have shouted out for pleasure, and must have done so but for the engrossing business of keeping a footing on the sloping ice with its soiled margin of yet more treacherous *moraine*. Yet on the glacier itself I was less handicapped than I had been on the way, and hopped along finely with my two shod sticks and the sharp new nails in my boots. Bob, however, was invariably in the van, and Mrs. Lascelles seemed more disposed to wait for me than to hurry after him. I think he pushed the pace unwittingly, under the prick of those emotions which otherwise were in such excellent control. I can see him now, continually waiting for us on the brow of some glistening ice-slope, leaning on his alpenstock and looking back, jet-black by contrast between the blinding hues of ice and sky.

But once he waited on the brink of some unfathomable crevasse, and then we all three cowered together and peeped down; the sides were green and smooth and sinister, like a crack in the sea, but so close together that one could not have fallen out of sight; yet when Bob loosened a lump of ice and kicked it in we heard it clattering from wall to wall in prolonged diminuendo before the faint splash just reached our ears. Mrs. Lascelles shuddered, and threw out a hand to prevent me from peering farther over. The gesture was obviously impersonal and instinctive, as an older eye would have seen, but Bob's was smouldering when mine met it next, and in the ensuing advance he left us farther behind than ever. But on the rock where we had our lunch he was once more himself, bright and boyish, careless and assured. So he continued till the end of that chapter. On the way home, moreover, he never once forged ahead, but was always ready with a hand for Mrs. Lascelles at the awkward places; and on the way through the woods, nothing would serve him but that I should set the pace, that we might all keep together. Judge therefore of my surprise when he came to my room, as I was dressing for the absurdly early dinner which is the one blot upon Riffel Alp arrangements, with the startling remark that we "might as well run straight with one another."

"By all means, my dear fellow," said I, turning to him with the lather on my chin. He was dressed already, as perfectly as usual, and his hands were in his pockets. But his fresh brown face was as grave as any judge's, and his mouth as stern. I went on to ask, disingenuously enough, if we had not been "running straight with each other" as it was.

"Not quite," said Bob Evers, dryly; "and we might as well, you know!"

"To be sure; but don't mind if I go on shaving, and pray speak for yourself."

"I will," he rejoined. "Do you remember our conversation the night you came?"

"More or less."

"I mean when you and I were alone together, before we turned in."

"Oh, yes. I remember something about it."

"It would be too silly to expect you to remember much," he went on after a pause, with a more delicate irony than heretofore. "But, as a matter of fact, I believe I said it was all rot that people talked about the impossibility of being mere pals with a woman, and all that sort of thing."

"I believe you did."

"Well, then, *that* was rot. That's all."

I turned round with my razor in mid-air,

"My dear fellow!" I exclaimed.

"Quite funny, isn't it?" he laughed, but rather harshly, while his mountain bronze deepened under my scrutiny.

"You are not in earnest, Bob!" said I; and on the word his laughter ended, his colour went.

"*I* am," he answered through his teeth. "*Are you?*"

Never was war carried more suddenly into the enemy's country, or that enemy's breath more completely taken away than mine. What could I say? "As much as you are, I should hope!" was what I ultimately said.

The lad stood raking me with a steady fire from his blue eyes.

"I mean to marry her," he said, "if she will have me."

There was no laughing at him. Though barely twenty, as I knew, he was man enough for any age as we faced each other in my room, and a man who knew his own mind into the bargain.

"But, my dear Bob," I ventured to remonstrate, "you are years too young—"

"That's my business. I am in earnest. What about you?"

I breathed again.

"My good fellow," said I, "you are at perfect liberty to give yourself away to me, but you really mustn't expect me to do quite the same for you."

"I expect precious little, I can tell you!" the lad rejoined hotly. "Not that it matters twopence so long as you are not misled by anything I said the other day. I prefer to run straight with you—you can run as you like with me. I only didn't want you to think that I was saying one thing and doing another. As a matter of fact I meant all I said at the time, or thought I did, until you came along and made me look into myself rather more closely than I had done before. I won't say how you managed it. You will probably see for yourself. But I'm very much obliged to you, whatever happens. And now that we understand each other there's no more to be said, and I'll clear out."

There was, indeed, no more to be said, and I made no attempt to detain him; for I did see for myself, only too clearly and precisely, how I had managed to precipitate the very thing which I had come out from England expressly to prevent.

CHAPTER VIII

PRAYERS AND PARABLES

I had quite forgotten one element which plays its part in most affairs of the affections. I mean, of course, the element of pique. Bob Evers, with the field to himself, had been sensible and safe enough; it was my intrusion, and nothing else, which had fanned his boyish flame into this premature conflagration. Of that I felt convinced. But Bob would not believe me if I told him so; and what else was there for me to tell him? To betray Catherine and the secret of my presence, would simply hasten an irrevocable step. To betray Mrs. Lascelles, and *her* secret, would certainly not prevent one. Both courses were out of the question upon other grounds. Yet what else was left?

To speak out boldly to Mrs. Lascelles, to betray Catherine and myself to her?

I shrank from that; nor had I any right to reveal a secret which was not only mine. What then was I to do? Here was this lad professedly on the point of proposing to this woman. It was useless to speak to the lad; it was impossible to speak to the woman. To be sure, she might not accept him; but the mere knowledge that she was to have the chance seemed enormously to increase my responsibility in the matter. As for the dilemma in which I now found myself, deservedly as you please, there was no comparing it with any former phase of this affair.

"O, what a tangled web we weave,
When first we practise to deceive!"

The hackneyed lines sprang unbidden, as though to augment my punishment; then suddenly I reflected that it was not in my own interest I had begun to practise my deceit; and the thought of Catherine braced me up, perhaps partly because I felt that it should. I put myself back into the fascinating little room in Elm Park Gardens. I saw the slender figure in the picture hat, I heard the half-humorous and half-pathetic voice. After all, it was for Catherine I had undertaken this ridiculous mission; she was therefore my first and had much better be my only consideration. I could not run with the hare after hunting with the hounds. And I should like to have seen Catherine's face if I had expressed any sympathy with the hare!

No; it was better to be unscrupulously stanch to one woman than weakly chivalrous toward both; and my mind was made up by the end of dinner. There was only one chance now of saving the wretched Bob, or rather one way of setting to work to save him; and that was by actually adopting the course with which he had already credited me. He thought I was "trying to cut him out." Well, I would try!

But the more I thought of him, of Mrs. Lascelles, of them both, the less sanguine I felt of success; for had I been she (I could not help admitting it to myself), as lonely, as reckless, as unlucky, I would have married the dear young idiot on the spot. Not that my own marriage (with Mrs. Lascelles) was an end that I contemplated for a moment as I took my cynical resolve. And now I trust that I have made both my position

E. W. Hornung

and my intentions very plain, and have written myself down neither more of a fool nor less of a knave than circumstances (and one's own infirmities) combined to make me at this juncture of my career.

The design was still something bolder than its execution, and if Bob did not propose that night it was certainly no fault of mine. I saw him with Mrs. Lascelles on the terrace after dinner; but I had neither the heart nor the face to thrust myself upon them. Everything was altered since Bob had shown me his hand; there were certain rules of the game which even I must now observe. So I left him in undisputed possession of the perilous ground, and being in a heavy glow from the strong air of the glacier, went early to my room; where I lay long enough without a wink, but quite prepared for Bob, with news of his engagement, at every step in the corridor.

Next day was Sunday, and chiefly, I am afraid, because there was neither blind nor curtain to my dormer-window, and the morning sun streamed full upon my pillow, I got up and went to early service in the little tin Protestant Church. It was wonderfully well attended. Quinby was there, a head taller than anybody else, and some sizes smaller in heads. The American bridegroom came in late with his "best girl." The late Vice Chancellor, with the peeled nose, and Mr. Belgrave Teale, fit for Church Parade, or for the afternoon act in one of his own fashion-plays, took round the offertory bags, into which Mr. Justice Sankey (in race-course checks) dropped gold. It was not the sort of service at which one cares to look about one, but I was among the early comers, and I could not help it. Mrs. Lascelles, however, was there before me, whereas Bob Evers was not there at all. Nevertheless, I did not mean to walk back with her until I saw her walking very much alone, a sort of cynosure even on the way from church, though humble and grave and unconscious as any country maid. I watched her with the rest, but in a spirit of my own. Some subtle change I seemed to detect in Mrs. Lascelles as in Bob. Had he really declared himself overnight, and had she actually accepted him? A new load seemed to rest upon her shoulders, a new anxiety, a new care; and as if to confirm my idea, she started and changed colour as I came up.

"I didn't see you in church," she remarked, in her own natural fashion, when we had exchanged the ordinary salutations.

"I am afraid you wouldn't expect to see me, Mrs. Lascelles."

"Well, as a matter of fact, I didn't, but I suppose," added Mrs. Lascelles, as her rich voice fell into a pensive (but not a pathetic) key, "I suppose it is you who are much more surprised at seeing me. I can't help it if you are, Captain Clephane. I am not really a religious person. I have not flown to that extreme as yet. But it has been a comfort to me, sometimes; and so, sometimes, I go."

It was very simply said, but with a sigh at the end that left me wondering whether she was in any new need of spiritual solace. Did she already find herself in the dilemma in which I had imagined her, and was it really a dilemma to her? New hopes began to chase my fears, and were gaining upon them when a flannel suit on the sunlit steps caused a temporary check: there was Bob waiting for us, his hands in his pockets, a smile upon his face, yet in the slope of his shoulders and the carriage of his head a certain indefinable but very visible attention and intent.

"Is Mrs. Evers a religious woman?" asked my companion, her step slowing ever so slightly as we approached.

"Not exactly; but she knows all about it," I replied.

"And doesn't believe very much? Then we shouldn't hit it off," exclaimed Mrs. Lascelles, "for I know nothing and believe all I can! Nevertheless, I'm not going to church again to-day."

The last words were in a sort of aside, and I afterwards heard that Bob and Mrs. Lascelles had attended the later service together on the previous Sunday; but I guessed almost as much on the spot, and it put out of my head both the unjust assumption of the earlier remark, concerning Catherine, and the contrast between them which Mrs. Lascelles could hardly afford to emphasise.

"Let's go somewhere else instead—Zermatt—or anywhere else you like," I suggested, eagerly; but we were close to the steps, and before she could reply Bob had taken off his straw hat to Mrs. Lascelles, and flung me a nod.

"How very energetic!" he cried. "I only hope it's a true indication of form, for I've got a scheme: instead of putting in another chapel I propose we stroll down to Zermatt for lunch and come back by the train."

Bob's proposal was made pointedly to Mrs. Lascelles, and as pointedly excluded me, but she stood between the two of us with a charming smile of good-humoured perplexity.

"Now what am I to say? Captain Clephane was in the very act of making the same suggestion!"

Bob glared on me for an instant in spite of Eton and all his ancestors.

"We'll all go together," I cried before he could speak. "Why not?"

Nor was this mere unreasoning or good-natured impulse, since Bob could scarcely have pressed his suit in my presence, while I should certainly have done my best to retard it; still, it was rather a relief to me to see him shake his head with some return of his natural grace.

"My idea was to show Mrs. Lascelles the gorge," said Bob, "but you can do that as well as I can; you can't miss it; besides, I've seen it, and I really ought to stay up here, as a matter of fact, for I'm on the track of a guide for the Matterhorn."

We looked at him narrowly with one accord, but he betrayed no signs of desperate impulse, only those of "climbing fever," and I at least breathed again.

"But if you want a guide," said I, "Zermatt's full of them."

"I know," said he, "but it's a particular swell I'm after, and he hangs out up here in the season. They expect him back from a big trip any moment, and I really ought to be on the spot to snap him up."

So Bob retired, in very fair order after all, and not without his laughing apologies to Mrs. Lascelles; but it was sad to me to note the spurious ring his laugh had now; it was like the death-knell of the simple and the single heart that it had been my lot, if not my mission, to poison and to warp. But the less said about my odious task, the sooner to its fulfilment, which now seemed close at hand.

It was not in fact so imminent as I supposed, for the descent into Zermatt is somewhat too steep for the conduct of a necessarily delicate debate. Sound legs go down at a compulsory run, and my companion was continually waiting for me to catch her up, only to shoot ahead again perforce.

E. W. Hornung

Or the path was too narrow for us to walk abreast, and you cannot become confidential in single file; or the noise of falling waters drowned our voices, when we stood together on that precarious platform in the cool depths of the gorge, otherwise such an admirable setting for the scene that I foresaw. Then it was a beautiful walk in itself, with its short tacks in the precipitous pine-woods above, its sudden plunge into the sunken gorge below, its final sweep across the green valley beyond; and it was all so new to us both that there were impressions to exchange or to compare at every turn. In fine, and with all the will in the world, it was quite impossible to get in a word about Bob before luncheon at the Monte Rosa, and by that time I for one was in no mood to introduce so difficult a topic.

But an opportunity there came, an opportunity such as even I could not neglect; on the contrary, I made too much of it, as the sequel will show. It was in the little museum which every tourist goes to see. We had shuddered over the gruesome relics of the first and worst catastrophe on the Matterhorn, and were looking in silence upon the primitive portraits of the two younger Englishmen who had lost their lives on that historic occasion. It appeared that they had both been about the same age as Bob Evers, and I pointed this out to my companion. It was a particularly obvious remark to make; but Mrs. Lascelles turned her face quickly to mine, and the colour left it in the half-lit, half-haunted little room, which we happened to have all to ourselves.

"Don't let him go up, Captain Clephane; don't let him, please!"

"Do you mean Bob Evers?" I asked, to gain time while I considered what to say; for the intensity of her manner took me aback.

"You know I do," said Mrs. Lascelles, impatiently; "don't let him go up the Matterhorn to-night, or to-morrow morning, or whenever it is that he means to start."

"But, my dear Mrs. Lascelles, who am I to prevent that young gentleman from doing what he likes?"

"I thought you were more or less related?"

"Rather less than more."

"But aren't you very intimate with his mother?"

I had to meet a pretty penetrating look.

"I was once."

"Well, then, for his mother's sake you ought to do your best to keep him out of danger, Captain Clephane."

It was my turn to repay the look which I had just received. No doubt I did so with only too much interest; no doubt I was equally clumsy of speech; but it was my opportunity, and something or other must be said.

"Quite so, Mrs. Lascelles; and for his mother's sake," said I, "I not only will do, I have already done, my best to keep the lad out of harm's way. He is the apple of her eye; they are simply all the world to one another. It would break her heart if anything happened to him—anything—if she were to lose him in any sense of the word."

I waited a moment, thinking she would speak, prepared on my side to be as explicit as she pleased; but Mrs. Lascelles only looked at me with her mouth tight shut and her eyes wide open; and I concluded—somewhat uneasily, I will confess—that she saw for herself what I meant.

"As for the Matterhorn," I went on, "that, I believe, is not such a very dangerous exploit in these days. There are permanent chains and things where there used to be polished precipices. It makes the real mountaineers rather scornful; anyone with legs and a head, they will tell you, can climb the Matterhorn nowadays. If I had the legs I'd go with him, like a shot."

"To share the danger, I suppose?"

"And the sport."

"Ah," said Mrs. Lascelles, "and the sport, of course! I had forgotten that!"

Yet I did not perceive that I had been found out, for nothing was further from my mind than to prolong the parable to which I had stooped in passing a few moments before. It had served its purpose, I conceived. I had given my veiled warning; it never occurred to me that Mrs. Lascelles might be indulging in a veiled retort. I thought she was annoyed at the hint that I had given her. I began to repent of that myself. It had quite spoilt our day, and so many and long were the silences, as we wandered from little shop to little shop, and finally with relief to the train, that I had plenty of time to remember how much we had found to talk about all the morning.

But matters were coming to a head in spite of me, for Bob Evers waylaid us on our return, and, with hardly a word to Mrs. Lascelles, straightway followed me to my room. He was pale with a suppressed anger which flared up even as he closed my door behind him, but though his honest face was now in flames, he still kept control of his tongue.

"I want you to lend me one of those sticks of yours," he said, quietly; "the heaviest, for choice."

"What the devil for?" I demanded, thinking for the moment of no shoulders but my own.

"To give that bounder Quinby the licking he deserves!" cried Bob: "to give it him now at once, when the post comes in, and there are plenty of people about to see the fun. Do you know what he's been saying and spreading all over the place?"

"No," I answered, my heart sinking within me. "What has he been saying?"

The colour altered on Bob's face, altered and softened to a veritable blush, and his eyes avoided mine.

"I'm ashamed to tell you, it makes me so sick," he said, disgustedly. "But the fact is that he's been spreading a report about Mrs. Lascelles; it has nothing on earth to do with me. It appears he only heard it himself this morning, by letter, but the brute has made good use of his time! *I* only got wind of it an hour or two ago, of course quite by accident, and I haven't seen the fellow since; but he's particularly keen on his letters, and either he explains himself to my satisfaction or I make an example of him before the hotel. It's a thing I never dreamt of doing in my life, and I'm sorry the poor beast is such a scarecrow; but it's a duty to punish that sort of crime against a woman, and now I'm sure you'll lend me one of your sticks. I am only sorry I didn't bring one with me."

"But wait a bit, my dear fellow," said I, for he was actually holding out his hand: "you have still to tell me what the report was."

E. W. Hornung

"Divorce!" he answered in a tragic voice. "Clephane, the fellow says she was divorced in India, and that it was—that it was her fault!"

He turned away his face. It was in a flame.

"And you are going to thrash Quinby for saying that?"

"If he sticks to it, I most certainly am," said Bob, the fire settling in his blue eyes.

"I should think twice about it, Bob, if I were you."

"My dear man, what else do you suppose I have been thinking of all the afternoon?"

"It will make a fresh scandal, you see."

"I can't help that."

And Bob shut his mouth with a self-willed snap.

"But what good will it do?"

"A liar will be punished, that's all! It's no use talking, Clephane; my mind is made up."

"But are you so sure that it's a lie?" I was obliged to say it at last, reluctantly enough, yet with a wretched feeling that I might just as well have said it in the beginning.

"Sure?" he echoed, his innocent eyes widening before mine. "Why, of course I'm sure! You don't know what pals we've been. Of course I never asked questions, but she's told me heaps and heaps of things; it would fit in with some of them, if it were true."

Then I told him that it was true, and how I knew that it was true, and my reason for having kept all that knowledge to myself until now. "I could not give her away even to you, Bob, nor yet tell you that I had known her before; for you would have been certain to ask when and how; and it was in her first husband's time, and under his name."

It was a comfort to be quite honest for once with one of them, and it is a relief even now to remember that I was absolutely honest with Bob Evers about this. He said almost at once that he would have done the same himself, and even as he spoke his whole manner changed toward me. His face had darkened at my unexpected confirmation of the odious rumour, but already it was beginning to lighten toward me, as though he found my attitude the one redeeming feature in the new aspect of affairs. He even thanked me for my late reserve, obviously from his heart, and in a way that went to mine on more grounds than one. It was as though a kindness to Mrs. Lascelles was already the greatest possible kindness to him.

"But I am glad you have told me now," he added, "for it explains many things. I was inclined to look upon you, Duncan—you won't mind my telling you now—as a bit of a deliberate interloper! But all the time you knew her first, and that alters everything. I hope to out you still, but I sha'n't any longer bear you a grudge if you out me!"

I was horrified.

"My dear fellow," I cried, "do you mean to say this makes no difference?"

"It does to Quinby. I must keep my hands off him, I suppose, though to my mind he deserves his licking all the more."

"But does it make no difference to *you*? My good boy, can you at your age seriously think of marrying a woman who has been married twice already, and divorced once?"

"I didn't know that when I thought of it first," he answered, doggedly, "and I am not going to let it make a difference now. Do you suppose I would stand away from her because of anything that's past and over? Do they stand away from us for—that sort of thing?"

Of course I said that was rather different, with as much conviction as though the ancient dogma had been my own.

"But, Duncan, you know it's the very last thing you're dreaming of doing yourself!"

And again I argued, as feebly as you please, that it was quite different in my case—that I was a good ten years older than he, and not my mother's only son.

Bob stiffened on the spot.

"My mother must take care of herself," said he; "and I," he added, "I must take care of myself, if you don't mind. And I hope you won't, for you've been most awfully good to me, you know! I never thought so until these last few minutes; but now I sha'n't forget it, no matter how it all turns out!"

CHAPTER IX

SUB JUDICE

Well, I made a belated attempt to earn my young friend's good opinion. I kept out of his way after dinner, and went in search of Quinby instead. I felt I had a crow of my own to pluck with this gentleman, who owed to my timely intervention a far greater immunity than he deserved. It was in the little billiard-room I found him, pachydermatously applauding the creditable attempts of Sir John Sankey at the cannon game, and as studiously ignoring the excellent shots of an undistinguished clergyman who was beating the judge. Quinby made room for me beside him, with a civility which might have caused me some compunction, but I repaid him by coming promptly to my point.

"What's this report about Mrs. Lascelles?" I asked, not angrily at all, for naturally my feeling in the matter was not so strong as Bob's, but with a certain contemptuous interest, if a man can judge of his own outward manner from his inner temper at the time.

Quinby favoured me with a narrow though a sidelong look; the room was very full, and in the general chit-chat, punctuated by the constant clicking of the heavy balls, there was very little danger of our being overheard. But Quinby was careful to lower his voice.

"It's perfectly true," said he, "if you mean about her being divorced."

"Yes, that was what I heard; but who started the report?"

"Who started it. You may well ask! Who starts anything in a place like this? Ah, good shot, Sir John, good shot!"

"Never mind the good shots, Quinby. I really rather want to talk to you about this. I sha'n't keep you long."

"Talk away, then. I am listening."

"Mrs. Lascelles and I are rather friends."

"So I can see."

"Very well, then, I want to know who started all this. It may be perfectly true, as you say, but who found it out? If you can't tell me I must ask somebody else."

The ruddy Alpine colouring had suddenly become accentuated in the case of Quinby.

"As a matter of fact," said he, "it was I who first heard of it, quite by chance. You can't blame me for that, Clephane."

"Of course not," said I encouragingly.

"Well, unfortunately I let it out; and you know how things get about in an hotel."

"It was unfortunate," I agreed. "But how on earth did you come to hear?"

Quinby hummed and hawed; he had heard from a soldier friend, a man who had known her in India, a man whom I knew myself, in fact Hamilton the sapper, who had telegraphed to Quinby to secure me my room. I ought to have been disarmed by the coincidence; but I recalled our initial conversation, about India and Hamilton and Mrs. Lascelles, and I could not consider it a coincidence at all.

"You don't mean to tell me," said I, aping the surprise I might have felt, "that our friend wrote and gave Mrs. Lascelles away to you of his own accord?"

But Quinby did not vouchsafe an answer. "Hard luck, Sir John!" cried he, as the judge missed an easy cannon, leaving his opponent a still easier one, which lost him the game. I proceeded to press my question in a somewhat stronger form, though still with all the suavity at my command.

"Surely," I urged, "you must have written to ask him about her first?"

"That's my business, I fancy," said Quinby, with a peculiarly aggressive specimen of the nasal snigger of which enough was made in a previous chapter, but of which Quinby himself never tired.

"Quite," I agreed; "but do you also consider it your business to inquire deliberately into the past life of a lady whom I believe you only know by sight, and to spread the result of your inquiries broadcast in the hotel? Is that your idea of chivalry? I shall ask Sir John Sankey whether it is his," I added, as the judge joined us with genial condescension, and I recollected that his proverbial harshness toward the male offender was redeemed by an extraordinary sympathy with the women. Thereupon I laid a general case before Sir John, asking him point-blank whether he considered such conduct as Quinby's (but I did not say whose the conduct was) either justifiable in itself or conducive to the enjoyment of a holiday community like ours.

"It depends," said the judge, cocking a critical eye on the now furious Quinby. "I am afraid we most of us enjoy our scandal, and for my part I always like to see a humbug catch it hot. But if the scandal's about a woman, and if it's an old scandal, and if she's a lonely woman, that quite alters the case, and in my opinion the author of it deserves all he gets."

At this Quinby burst out, with an unrestrained heat that did not lower him in my estimation, though the whole of his tirade was directed exclusively against me. I had been talking "at" him, he declared. I might as well have been straightforward while I was about it. He, for his part, was not afraid to take the responsibility for anything he might have said. It was perfectly true, to begin with. The so-called Mrs. Lascelles, who was such a friend of mine, had been the wife of a German Jew in Lahore, who had divorced her on her elopement with a Major Lascelles, whom she had left in his turn, and whose name she had not the smallest right to bear. Quinby exercised some restraint in the utterances of these calumnies, or the whole room must have heard them, but even as it was we had more listeners than the judge when my turn came.

"I won't give you the lie, Quinby, because I am quite sure you don't know you are telling one," said I; "but as a matter of fact you are giving currency to two. In the first place, this lady is Mrs. Lascelles, for the major did marry her; in the second place, Major Lascelles is dead."

"And how do you know?" inquired Quinby, with a touch of genuine surprise to mitigate an insolent disbelief.

"You forget," said I, "that it was in India I knew your own informant. I can only say that my information in all this matter is a good deal better than his. I knew Mrs. Lascelles herself quite well out there; I knew the other side of her case. It doesn't seem to have struck you, Quinby, that such a woman must have suffered a good deal before, and after, taking such a step. Or I don't suppose you would have spread yourself to make her suffer a little more,"

And I still consider that a charitable view of his behaviour; but Quinby was of another opinion, which he expressed with his offensive little laugh as he lifted his long body from the settee.

"This is what one gets for securing a room for a man one doesn't know!" said he.

"On the contrary," I retorted, "I haven't forgotten that, and I have saved you something because of it. I happen to have saved you no less than a severe thrashing from a stronger man than myself, who is even more indignant with you than I am, and who wanted to borrow one of my sticks for the purpose!"

"And it would have served him perfectly right," was the old judge's comment, when the mischief-maker had departed without returning my parting shot. "I suppose you meant young Evers, Captain Clephane?"

"I did indeed, Sir John. I had to tell him the truth in order to restrain him."

The old judge raised his eyebrows.

"Then you hadn't to tell him it before? You are certainly consistent, and I rather admire your position as regards the lady. But I am not so sure that it was altogether fair toward the lad. It is one thing to stand up for the poor soul, my dear sir, but it would be another thing to let a nice boy like that go and marry her!"

So that was the opinion of this ripe old citizen of the world! It ought not to have irritated me as it did. It would be Catherine's opinion, of course; but a dispassionate view was not to be expected from her. I had not hitherto thought otherwise, myself; but now I experienced a perverse inclination to take the opposite side. Was it so utterly impossible for a woman with this woman's record to make a good wife to some man yet? I did not admit it for an instant; he would be a lucky man who won so healthy and so good a heart; thus I argued to myself with Mrs. Lascelles in my mind, and nobody else. But Bob Evers was not a man, I was not sure that he was out of his teens, and to think of him was to think at once with Sir John Sankey and all the rest. Yes, yes, it would be madness and suicide in such a youth; there could be no two opinions about that; and yet I felt indignant at the mildest expression of that which I myself could not deny.

Such was my somewhat chaotic state of mind when I had fled the billiard-room in my turn, and put on my overcoat and cap to commune with myself outside. Nobody did justice to Mrs. Lascelles; it was terribly hard to do her justice; those were perhaps the ideas that were oftenest uppermost. I did not see how I was to be the exception and prove the rule; my brief was for Bob, and there was an end of it. It was foolish to worry, especially on such a night. The moon had waxed since my arrival, and now hung almost round and altogether dazzling in the little sky the mountains left us. Yet I had the terrace all to myself; the magnificent voice of our latest celebrity had drawn everybody else in doors, or under the open drawing-room windows through which it poured out into the glorious night. And in the vivid moonlight the very mountains seemed to have gathered about the little human hive upon their heights, to be listening to the grand rich notes that had some right to break their ancient silence.

"If doughty deeds my lady please,
Right soon I'll mount my steed;
And strong his arm, and fast his seat,
That bears frae me the meed.
I'll wear thy colours in my cap,
Thy picture at my heart;
And he that bends not to thine eye
Shall rue it to his smart!"

It was a brave new setting to brave old lines, as simple and direct as themselves, studiously in keeping, passionate, virile, almost inspired; and the whole so justly given that the great notes did not drown the words as they often will, but all came clean to the ear. No wonder the hotel held its breath! I was standing entranced myself, an outpost of the audience underneath the windows, whose fringe I could just see round the uttermost angle of the hotel, when Bob Evers ran down the steps, and came toward me in such guise that I could not swear to him till the last yard.

"Don't say a word," he whispered excitedly. "I'm just off!"

"Off where?" I gasped, for he had changed into full mountaineering garb, and there was his greased face beaming in the moonlight, and the blue spectacles twinkling about his hatband, at half-past nine at night.

"Up the Matterhorn!"

"At this time of night?"

E. W. Hornung

"It is a bit late, and that's why I want it kept quiet. I don't want any fuss or advice. I've got a couple of excellent guides waiting for me just below by the shoemaker's hut. I told you I was on their tracks. Well, it was to-night or never as far as they were concerned, they are so tremendously full up. So to-night it is, and don't you remind me of my mother!"

I was thinking of her when he spoke; for the song had swung through a worthy refrain into another verse, and now I knew it better. It was Catherine who had introduced me to all my lyrics; it was to Catherine I had once hymned this one in my unformed heart.

"But I thought," said I, as I forced myself to think, "that everybody went up to the *Cabane* overnight, and started fresh from there in the morning?"

"Most people do, but it's as broad as it's long," declared Bob, airily, rapidly, and with the same unwonted excitement, born as I thought of his unwonted enterprise. "You have a ripping moonlight walk instead of a so-called night's rest in a frowsy hut. We shall get our breakfast there instead, and I expect to start fresher than if I had slept there and been knocked up at two o'clock in the morning. That's all settled, anyhow, and you can look for me on top through the telescope after breakfast. I shall be back before dark, and then—"

"Well, what then?" I asked, for Bob had made a significant and yet irresolute pause, as though he could not quite bring himself to tell me something that was on his mind.

"Well," he echoed nonchalantly at last, as though he had not hesitated at all, "as a matter of fact, to-morrow night I am to know my fate. I have asked Mrs. Lascelles to marry me, and she hasn't said no, but I am giving her till to-morrow night. That's all, Clephane. I thought it a fair thing to let you know.

If you want to waltz in and try your luck while I'm gone, there's nothing on earth to prevent you, and it might be most satisfactory to everybody. As a matter of fact, I'm only going so as to get over the time and keep out of the way."

"As a matter of fact?" I queried, waving a little stick toward the lighted windows. "Listen a minute, and then tell me!"

And we listened together to the last and clearest rendering of the refrain—

"Then tell me how to woo thee, Love;
O tell me how to woo thee!
For thy dear sake, nae care I'll take,
Tho' ne'er another trow me!"

"What tosh!" shouted Bob (his mother should have heard him) through the applause. "Of course I'm going to take care of myself, and of course I meant to rush the Matterhorn while I'm here, but between ourselves that's my only reason for rushing it to-night."

Yet had he no boyish vision of quick promotion in the lady's heart, no primitive desire to show his mettle out of hand, to set her trembling while he did or died? He had, I thought, and he had not; that shining face could only have reflected a single and candid heart. But it is these very natures, so simple and sweet-hearted and transparent, that are least to be trusted on the subject of their own motives and emotions, for they are the soonest deceived, not only by others but in themselves. Or so I venture to think, and even then reflected, as I shook my dear lad's hand by the side parapet of the moonlit terrace, and watched him run down into the shadows of the fir-trees and so out of my sight with two dark and stalwart figures that promptly detached themselves from the shadows of the shoemaker's hut. A third figure mounted to where I now sat listening to the easy, swinging, confident steps, as they fell fainter and fainter upon the ear; it was the shoemaker himself who had shod my two sticks with spikes and my boots with formidable nails; and we exchanged a few words in a mixture of languages which I should be very sorry to reproduce.

"Do you know those two guides?" is what I first asked in effect.

"Very well, monsieur."

"Are they good guides?"

"The very best, monsieur."

CHAPTER X

THE LAST WORD

"Is that you?"

It was an hour or so later, but still I sat ruminating upon the parapet, within a yard or two of the spot where I had first accosted Bob Evers and Mrs. Lascelles. I had retraced the little sequence of subsequent events, paltry enough in themselves, yet of a certain symmetry and some importance as a whole. I had attacked and defended my own conduct down to that hour, when I ought to have been formulating its logical conclusion, and during my unprofitable deliberations the night had aged and altered (as it were) behind my back. There was no more music in the drawing-room. There were no more people under the drawing-room windows. The lights in all the lower windows were not what they had been; it was the bedroom tiers that were illuminated now. But I did not realise that there was less light outside until I awoke to the fact that Mrs. Lascelles was peering tentatively toward me, and putting her question in such an uncertain tone.

"That depends who I am supposed to be," I answered, laughing as I rose to put my personality beyond doubt.

"How stupid of me!" laughed Mrs. Lascelles in her turn,

E. W. Hornung

though rather nervously to my fancy. "I thought it was Mr. Evers!"

I had hard work to suppress an exclamation. So he had not told her what he was going to do, and yet he had not forbidden me to tell her. Poor Bob was more subtle than I had supposed, but it was a simple subtlety, a strange chord but still in key with his character as I knew it.

"I am sorry to disappoint you," said I. "But I am afraid you won't see any more of Bob Evers to-night."

"What do you mean?" asked Mrs. Lascelles, suspiciously.

"I wonder he didn't tell you," I replied, to gain time in which to decide how to make the best use of such an unforeseen opportunity.

"Well, he didn't; so please will you, Captain Clephane?"

"Bob Evers," said I, with befitting gravity, "is climbing the Matterhorn at this moment."

"Never!"

"At least he has started."

"When did he start?"

"An hour or more ago, with a couple of guides."

"He told you, then?"

"Only just as he was starting."

"Was it a sudden idea?"

"More or less, I think."

I waited for the next question, but that was the last of them. Just then the interloping cloud floated clear of the moon, and I saw that my companion was wrapped up as on the earlier night, in the same unconventional combination of rain-coat and golf-cape; but now the hood hung down, and the sudden rush of moonlight showed me a face as full of sheer perplexity and annoyance as I could have hoped to find it, and as free from deeper feeling.

"The silly boy!" exclaimed Mrs. Lascelles at last. "I suppose it really is pretty safe, Captain Clephane?"

"Safer than most dangerous things, I believe; and they are the safest, as you know, because you take most care. He has a couple of excellent guides; the chance of getting them was partly why he went. In all human probability we shall have him back safe and sound, and fearfully pleased with himself, long before this time to-morrow. Meanwhile, Mrs. Lascelles," I continued with the courage of my opportunity, "it is a very good chance for me to speak to you about our friend Bob. I have wanted to do so for some little time."

"Have you, indeed?" said Mrs. Lascelles, coldly.

"I have," I answered imperturbably; "and if it wasn't so late I should ask for a hearing now."

"Oh, let us get it over, by all means!"

But as she spoke Mrs. Lascelles glanced over the shoulder that she shrugged so contemptuously, toward the lights in the bedroom windows, most of which were wide open.

"We could walk toward the zig-zags," I suggested. "There is

E. W. Hornung

a seat within a hundred yards, if you don't think it too cold to sit, but in any case I needn't keep you many minutes. Bob Evers," I continued, as my suggestion was tacitly accepted, "paid me the compliment of confiding in me somewhat freely before he started on this hare-brained expedition of his."

"So it appears."

"Ah, but he didn't only tell me what he was going to do; he told me why he was doing it," said I, as we sauntered on our way side by side. "It was difficult to believe," I added, when I had waited long enough for the question upon which I had reckoned.

"Indeed?"

"He said he had proposed to you."

And again I waited, but never a word.

"That child!" I added with deliberate scorn.

But a further pause was broken only by my companion's measured steps and my own awkward shuffle.

"That baby!" I insisted.

"Did you tell him he was one, Captain Clephane?" asked Mrs. Lascelles, dryly, but drawn so far at last.

"I spared his feelings. But can it be true, Mrs. Lascelles?"

"It is true."

"Is it a fact that you didn't give him a definite answer?"

"I don't know what business it is of yours," said Mrs. Lascelles, bluntly; "and since he seems to have told you everything, neither do I know why you should ask me. However, it is quite true that I did not finally refuse him on the spot."

This carefully qualified confirmation should have afforded me abundant satisfaction. I was over-eager in the matter, however, and I cried out impetuously:

"But you will?"

"Will what?"

"Refuse the boy!"

We had reached the seat, but neither of us sat down. Mrs. Lascelles appeared to be surveying me with equal resentment and defiance. I, on the other hand, having shot my bolt, did my best to look conciliatory.

"Why should I refuse him?" she asked at length, with less emotion and more dignity than her bearing had led me to expect. "You seem so sure about it, you know!"

"He is such a boy—such an utter child—as I said just now." I was conscious of the weakness of saying it again, and it alone, but my strongest arguments were too strong for direct statement.

This one, however, was not unfruitful in the end.

"And I," said Mrs. Lascelles, "how old do you think I am? Thirty-five?"

"Of course not," I replied, with obvious gallantry. "But I

doubt if Bob is even twenty."

"Well, then, you won't believe me, but I was married before I was his age, and I am just six-and-twenty now."

It was a surprise to me. I did not doubt it for a moment; one never did doubt Mrs. Lascelles. It was indeed easy enough to believe (so much I told her) if one looked upon the woman as she was, and only difficult in the prejudicial light of her matrimonial record. I did not add these things. "But you are a good deal older," I could not help saying, "in the ways of the world, and it is there that Bob is such an absolute infant."

"But I thought an Eton boy was a man of the world?" said Mrs. Lascelles, quoting me against myself with the utmost readiness.

"Ah, in some things," I had to concede. "Only in some things, however."

"Well," she rejoined, "of course I know what you mean by the other things. They matter to your mind much more than mere age, even if I had been fifteen years older, instead of five or six. It's the old story, from the man's point of view. You can live anything down, but you won't let us. There is no fresh start for a woman; there never was and never will be."

I protested that this was unfair. "I never said that, or anything like it, Mrs. Lascelles!"

"No, you don't say it, but you think it!" she cried back. "It is the one thing you have in your mind. I was unhappy, I did wrong, so I can never be happy, I can never do right! I am unfit to marry again, to marry a good man, even if he loves me, even if I love him!"

"I neither say nor think anything of the kind," I reiterated, and with some slight effect this time. Mrs. Lascelles put no more absurdities into my mouth.

"Then what do you say?" she demanded, her deep voice vibrant with scornful indignation, though there were tears in it too.

"I think he will be a lucky fellow who gets you," I said, and meant every word, as I looked at her well in the moonlight, with her shining eyes, and curling lip, and fighting flush.

"Thank you, Captain Clephane!"

And I thought I was to be honoured with a contemptuous courtesy; but I was not.

"He ought to be a man, however," I went on, "and not a boy, and still less the only child of a woman with whom you would never get on."

"So you are as sure of that," exclaimed Mrs. Lascelles, "as of everything else!" It seemed, however, to soften her, or at least to change the current of her thoughts. "Yet you get on with her?" she added with a wistful intonation.

I could not deny that I got on with Catherine Evers.

"You are even fond of her?"

"Quite fond."

"Then do you find me a very disagreeable person, that she and I couldn't possibly hit it off, in your opinion?"

"It isn't that, Mrs. Lascelles," said I, almost wearily. "You must know what it is. You want to marry her son—"

Mrs. Lascelles smiled.

"Well, let us suppose you do. That would be quite enough for Mrs. Evers. No matter who you were, how peerless, how incomparable in every way, she would rather die than let you marry him at his age. I don't say she's wrong—I don't say she's right. I give you the plain fact for what it is worth: you would find her from the first a clever and determined adversary, a regular little lioness with her cub, and absolutely intolerant on that particular point."

I could see Catherine as I spoke, the Catherine I had seen last, and liked least to remember; but the vision faded before the moonlit reality of Mrs. Lascelles, laughing to herself like˙ a great, naughty, pretty child.

"I really think I must marry him," she said, "and see what happens!"

"If you do," I answered, in all seriousness, "you will begin by separating mother and son, and end by making both their lives miserable, and bringing the last misery into your own."

And either my tone impressed her, or the covert reminder in my last words; for the bold smile faded from her face, and she looked longer and more searchingly in mine than she had done as yet.

"You know Mrs. Evers exceedingly well," Mrs. Lascelles remarked.

"I did years ago," I guardedly replied.

"Do you mean to say," urged my companion, "that you have

not seen her for years?"

I did not altogether like her tone. Yet it was so downright and straightforward, it was hard to be the very reverse in answer to it, and I shied idiotically at the honest lie. I had quite lost sight both of Bob and his mother, I declared, from the day I went to India until now.

"You mean until you came out here?" persisted Mrs. Lascelles.

"Until the other day," I said, relying on a carefully affirmative tone to close the subject. There was a pause. I began to hope I had succeeded. The flattering tale was never finished.

"I believe," said Mrs. Lascelles, "that you saw Mrs. Evers in town before you started."

It was too late to lie.

"As a matter of fact," I answered easily, "I did."

I built no hopes on the pause which followed that. Somehow I had my face to the moon, and Mrs. Lascelles had her back. Yet I knew that her scrutiny of me was more critical than ever.

"How funny of Bob never to have told me!" she said.

"Told you what?"

"That you saw his mother just before you left."

"I didn't tell him," I said at length.

E. W. Hornung

"That was funny of you, Captain Clephane."

"On the contrary," I argued, with the impudence which was now my only chance, "it was only natural. Bob was rather raw with his friend Kennerley, you see. You knew about that?"

"Oh, yes."

"And why they fell out?"

"Yes."

"Well, he might have thought the other fellow had been telling tales, and that I had come out to have an eye on him, if he had known that I happened to see his mother just before I started."

There was another pause; but now I was committed to an attitude, and prepared for the worst.

"Perhaps there would have been some truth in it?" suggested Mrs. Lascelles.

"Perhaps," I agreed, "a little."

The pause now was the longest of all. It had no terrors for me. Another cloud had come between us and the moon. I was sorry for that. I felt that I was missing something. Even the fine upstanding figure before me was no longer sharp enough to be expressive.

"I have been harking back," explained Mrs. Lascelles, eventually. "Now I begin to follow. You saw his mother, you heard a report, and you volunteered or at least consented to come out and keep an eye on the dear boy, as you say yourself. Am I not more or less right so far, Captain Clephane?"

Her tone was frozen honey.

"More or less," I admitted ironically.

"Of course, I don't know what report that other miserable young man may have carried home with him. I don't want to know. But I can guess. One does not stay in hotel after hotel without getting a pretty shrewd idea of the way people talk about one. I know the sort of things they have been saying here. You would hear them yourself, no doubt, Captain Clephane, as soon as you arrived."

I admitted that I had, but reminded Mrs. Lascelles that the first person I had spoken to was also the greatest gossip in the hotel. She paid no attention to the remark, but stood looking at me again, with the look that I could never quite see to read.

"And then," she went on, "you found out who it was, and you remembered all about me, and your worst fears were confirmed. That must have been an interesting moment. I wonder how you felt.... Did it never occur to you to speak plainly to anybody?"

"I wasn't going to give you away," I said, stolidly, though with no conscious parade of virtue.

"Yet, you see, it would have made no difference if you had! Did you seriously think it would make much difference, Captain Clephane, to a really chivalrous young man?" I bowed my head to the well-earned taunt. "But," she went on, "there was no need for you to speak to Mr. Evers. You might have spoken to me. Why did you not do that?"

"Because I didn't want to quarrel with you," I answered quite honestly; "because I enjoyed your society too much myself."

"That was very nice of you," said Mrs. Lascelles, with a sudden although subtle return of the good-nature which had always attracted me. "If it is sincere," she added, as an apparent afterthought.

"I am perfectly sincere now."

"Then what do you think I should do?" she asked me, in the soft new tone which actually flattered me with the idea that she was making up her mind to take my advice.

"Refuse this lad!"

"And then?" she almost whispered.

"And then—"

I hesitated. I found it hard to say what I thought, hard even upon myself. We had been good friends. I admired the woman cordially; her society was pleasant to me, as it always had been. Nevertheless, we had just engaged in a duel of no friendly character; and now that we seemed of a sudden to have become friends again, it was the harder to give her the only advice which I considered compatible alike with my duty and the varied demands of the situation. If she took it as she seemed disposed to do, the immediate loss would be mine, and I foresaw besides a much more disagreeable reckoning with Bob Evers than the one now approaching an amicable conclusion. I should have to stay behind to face the music of his wrath alone. Still, at the risk of appearing brutal I made my proposal in plain terms; but, to minimise that risk, I ventured to take the lady's hand and was glad to find the familiarity permitted in the same friendly spirit in which it was indulged.

"I would have no 'and then,'" I said, "if I were you. I should refuse him under such circumstances that he couldn't possibly bother you, or himself about you, again. Now is your opportunity."

"Is it?" she asked, a thrilling timbre in her low voice. And I fancied there was a kindred tremor in the firm warm hand within mine.

"The best of opportunities," I replied, "if you are not too wedded to this place, and can tear yourself away from the rest of us." (Her hand lay loose in mine.) "Mrs. Lascelles, I should go to-morrow morning" (her hand fell away altogether), "while he is still up the Matterhorn and I shouldn't let him know where I—shouldn't give him a chance of finding out—"

A sudden peal of laughter cut me short. I could not have believed it came from my companion. But no other soul was near us, though I looked all ways. It was the merriest laughter imaginable, only the merriment was harsh and hard.

"Oh, thank you, Captain Clephane! You are too delicious! I saw it coming; I only wondered whether I could contain myself until it came. Yet I could hardly believe that even you would commit yourself to that finishing touch of impudence! Certainly it is an opportunity, *his* being out of the way. *you* were not long in making use of it, were you? It will amuse him when he comes down, though it may open his eyes. I shall tell him everything, so I give you warning. Every single thing, that you have had the insolence to tell me!"

She had caught up her skirts from the ground, she had half turned away from me, toward the hotel. The false merriment

E. W. Hornung

had died out of her. The true indignation remained, ringing in every accent of the deep sweet voice, and drawn up in every inch of the tall straight figure. I do not remember whether the moon was hid or shining at the moment. I only know that my lady's eyes shone bright enough for me to see them then and ever after, bright and dry with a scorn that burnt too hot for tears; and that I admired her even while she scorned me, as I had never thought to admire any woman but one, but this woman least of all.

So we both stood, intent, some seconds, looking our last upon each other if I was wise. Then I lifted my hat, and offered my congratulations (more sincere than they sounded) to her and Bob.

"Did I tell you why he is going up?" I added. "It is to pass the time until he knows his fate. If only we could let him know it now!"

Mrs. Lascelles glanced toward the mountain, and my eyes followed hers. A great cloud hid the grim outstanding summit.

"If only you had prevented him from going!" she cried back at me in a last reproach; and to me her tone was conclusive, it rang so true, and so invidiously free from the smaller emotions which it had been my own unhappiness to inspire. It was the real woman who had spoken out once more, suddenly, perhaps unthinkingly, but obviously from her heart. And as she turned, I followed her very slowly and without a word; for now was I surely and deservedly undone.

CHAPTER XI

THE LION'S MOUTH

It was a chilly morning, with rather a high wind; from the haze about the mountains of the Zermatt valley, which were all that I could see from my bedroom window, it occurred to me that I might look in vain for the Matterhorn from the other side of the hotel. It was still visible, however, when I came down, a white cloud wound about its middle like a cloth, and the hotel telescope already trained upon its summit from the shelter of the glass veranda.

"See anybody?" I asked of a man who sat at the telescope as though his eye was frozen to the lens. He might have been witnessing the most exciting adventure, where the naked eye saw only rock and snow, and cold grey sky; but he rose at last with a shake of the head, a great gaunt man with kind keen eyes, and the skin peeled off his nose.

"No," said he, "I can't see anybody, and I'm very glad I can't. It's about as bad a morning for it as you could possibly have; yet last night was so fine that some fellows might have got up to the hut, and been foolish enough not to come down again. But have a look for yourself."

"Oh, thanks," said I, considerably relieved at what I heard, "but if you can't see anybody I'm sure I can't. You have done it yourself, I daresay?"

The gaunt man smiled demurely, and the keen eyes twinkled in his flayed face. He was, indeed, a palpable mountaineer.

"What, the Matterhorn?" said he, lowering his voice and looking about him as if on the point of some discreditable admission. "Oh, yes, I've done the Matterhorn, back and front and both sides, with and without guides; but everybody has, in these days. It's nothing when you know the ropes and chains and things. They've got everything up there now except an iron staircase. Still, I should be sorry to tackle it to-day, even if they had a lift!"

"Do you think guides would?" I asked, less reassured than I had felt at first.

"It depends on the guides. They are not the first to turn back, as a rule; but they like wind and mist even less than we do. The guides know what wind and mist mean."

I now understood the special disadvantages of the day and realised the obvious dangers. I could only hope that either Bob Evers or his guides had shown the one kind of courage required by the occasion, the moral courage of turning back. But I was not at all sure of Bob. His stimulus was not that of the single-minded, level-headed mountaineer; in his romantic exaltation he was capable of hailing the very perils as so many more means of grace in the sight of Mrs. Lascelles; yet without doubt he would have repudiated any such incentive, and that in all the sincerity of his simple heart. He did not know himself as I knew him.

My fears were soon confirmed. Returning to the glass veranda, after the stock breakfast of the Swiss hotel, with its horseshoe rolls and fabricated honey, I found the telescope the centre of an ominous crowd, on whose fringe hovered my new friend the mountaineer.

"We were wrong," he muttered to me. "Some fools are up there, after all."

"How many?" I asked quickly.

"I don't know. There's no getting near the telescope now, and won't be till the clouds blot them out altogether."

I looked out at the Matterhorn. The loincloth of cloud had shaken itself out into a flowing robe, from which only the brown skull of the mountain protruded in its white skull-cap.

"There are three of them," announced a nasal voice from the heart of the little crowd. "A great long chap and two guides."

"He can't possibly know that," remarked the mountaineer to me, "but let's hope it is so."

"They're as plain as pike-staffs," continued Quinby, whose bent blond head I now distinguished, as he occupied the congenial post of Sister Anne. "They seem stuck.... No, they're getting up on to the snow-slope, and the front man's cutting steps."

"Then they're all right for the present," said the mountaineer. "It's the getting down that's ticklish."

"You can see the rope blowing about between them ... what a wind there must be ... it's bent out taut like a bow, you can see it against the snow, and they're bending themselves more than forty-five degrees to meet it."

E. W. Hornung

"All very well going *up*," murmured the mountaineer: there was a sinister innuendo in the curt comments of the practical man.

I turned into the hall. It, however, was quite deserted. I had hoped I might see something of Mrs. Lascelles; she was not one of those in the glass veranda. I now looked in the drawing-room, but neither was she there. Returning to the empty hall, I passed a minute peering through the locked glass door of the pigeon-holes in which the careful concierge files the unclaimed letters. There was nothing for me that I could discern, in the C pigeon-hole; but next door but one, under E, there lay on the very top a letter which caught my eye and more. It had not been through any post. It was a note directed to R. Evers, Esq., in a hand that I knew instinctively to be that of Mrs. Lascelles, though I had never seen it in my life before. It was a good hand, but large and bold and downright as herself.

The concierge stood in the doorway, one eye on the disappearing Matterhorn, one on the experts and others in animated conclave round the still inaccessible telescope. I touched the concierge on the arm.

"Did you see Mrs. Lascelles this morning?"

The man's eyes opened before his lips.

"She has gone away, sir."

"I know," I said, having indeed divined no less. "What train did she catch?"

"The first one from here. That also catches the early train from Zermatt."

"I am sorry," I said after a pause. "I hoped to see Mrs. Lascelles before she went; now I must write. She left you an address, I suppose?"

"Oh, yes, sir."

"I shall ask you for it later on. No letters for me, I suppose?"

"No, sir."

"Sure?"

"I will look again."

And I looked with him, over his shoulder; but there was nothing; and the note for Bob Evers now inspired me with a tripartite blend of curiosity, envy, and apprehension. I would have had a last word from the same hand myself; had it been never so scornful, this silent scorn was the harder sort to bear. Also I wanted much to know what her last word was to Bob—and dreaded more what it might be.

There remained the unexpected triumph of having got rid of my lady after all. That is not to be belittled even now. It is a triumph to succeed in any undertaking, more especially when one has abandoned one's own last hope of such success. The unpleasant character of this particular emprise made its eventual accomplishment in some ways the greater matter for congratulation in my eyes. At least I had done my part. I had come to hate it, but the thing was done, and it had been a fairly difficult thing to do. It was impossible not to plume oneself a little on the whole, but the feeling was a superficial one, with deeper and uneasier feelings underneath. Still, I had practically redeemed my impulsive promise to Catherine Evers; her son and this woman once parted, it should be easy to keep them apart, and my knowledge of the woman forbade me to deny the fullest significance to her departure. She had gone away to stay away—from Bob. She had listened to me the less with her ears, because her reason and her heart had been compelled to heed. To be sure, she saw the unsuitability, the impossibility, as clearly as we did. But it was I who, at all events, had helped to make her see it; wherefore I deserved well of Catherine Evers, if of no other person in the world.

Oddly enough, this last consideration afforded me least satisfaction; it seemed to bring home to me by force of contrast the poor figure that I must assuredly cut in the eyes of the other two, the still poorer opinion that they would have of me if ever they knew all. I did not care to pursue this train of thought. It was a subject upon which I was not prepared to examine myself; to change it, I thought of Bob's present peril, which I had almost forgotten as I lounged abstractedly in the empty hall. If anything were to happen to him, in the vulgar sense! What an irony, what poetic punishment for us survivors! And yet, even as I rehearsed the ghastly climax in my mind, I told myself that the mother would rather see him even thus, than married to a widow who had also been divorced; it was the younger woman who would never forgive me, or herself.

Disappointed faces met me on my next visit to the veranda. The little crowd there had dwindled to a group. I could have had the telescope now for as long as I liked: the upper part of the Matterhorn was finally and utterly effaced and swallowed up by dense white mist and cloud. My friend the mountaineer looked grave, but his disfigured face did not wear the baulked expression of others to which he drew my attention.

"It is like the curtain coming down with the man's head still in the lion's mouth," said he.

"I hope," said I devoutly, "that you don't seriously think there's any analogy?"

The climber looked at me steadily, and then smiled.

"Well, no, perhaps I don't think it quite so bad as all that. But it's no use pretending it isn't dangerous. May I ask if you know who the foolhardy fellow is?"

I said I did not know, but mentioned my suspicion, only begging my climbing friend not to let the name go any farther. It was in too many mouths already, in quite another connection, I was going on to explain; but the mountaineer nodded, as much as to warn me that even he knew all about that. It was Bob's office, however, to provide the hotel with its sensation while he remained, and he was not allowed to perform anonymously very long. His departure over night leaked out. I was asked if it was true. The flight of Mrs. Lascelles was the next discovery; desperate deductions were drawn at once. She had jilted the unlucky youth and sent him in utter recklessness on his intentionally suicidal ascent. Nobody any longer expected to see him come down alive; so much I gathered from the fragments of conversation that reached my ears; and never was better occupation for a bad day than appeared to be afforded by the discussion of the supposititious tragedy in all its imaginary details. As, however, the talk invariably abated at my approach, giving place to uncomplimentary glances in my direction, I could not but infer that public opinion had assigned me an unenviable part in the piece. Perhaps I deserved it, though not from their point of view.

The afternoon was at once a dreariness and a dread. There was no ray of sun without, no sort of warmth within. The Matterhorn never reappeared, but seemed the grimmer monster for this sinister invisibility. I gathered that there was

E. W. Hornung

real occasion for anxiety, if not for alarm, and I nursed mine chiefly in my own room until I heard the news when I went down for my letters. Bob Evers had walked in as though nothing had happened, and gone straight up to his room with a note that the concierge handed him. Some one had asked him whether it was he who had been up the Matterhorn in the morning, and young Evers had vouchsafed the barest affirmative compatible with civility. The sunburnt climber was my informant.

"And I don't mind telling you it is a relief to me," he added, "and to everybody, though I shouldn't wonder if there was a little unconscious disappointment in the air as well. I congratulate you, for I could see you were anxious, and I must find an opportunity of congratulating your young friend himself."

Meanwhile no such opportunity was afforded me, though I quite expected and was fully prepared for another visit from Bob in my room. I waited for him there until dinner-time, but he never came, and I was beginning to wish he would. It was like the wrapping of the Matterhorn in mist; it only widened the field of apprehension; and yet it was not for me to go to the boy. My unrest was further aggravated by a letter which I had just received from the boy's mother in answer to my first to her. It was not a very dreadful letter; but I only trusted that no evil impulse had caused Catherine to write in anything like the same strain to Bob; for neither was it a very charitable letter, nor one that a man could be glad to get from the woman whom he had set out on an enduring pinnacle. There was only this to be said for it, that years ago I had sought in vain for a really human weakness in Catherine Evers, and now at last I had found one. She was rather too human about Mrs. Lascelles.

I looked for Bob both at and after dinner, but we were never within speaking distance and I fancied he avoided even my eye. What had Mrs. Lascelles said? He looked redder and browner and rougher in the face, but I heard that he would hardly open his lips at table, that he was almost surly on the subject of his exploit. Everybody else appeared to me to be speaking of it, or of Bob himself; but I had him on my nerves and may well have formed an exaggerated impression about it all. Only I do not forget some of the things I did overhear that day, and night; and they now had the effect of sending me in search of Bob, since Bob would not come near me. "I will have it out with him," I grimly decided, "and then get out of this myself by the first train going." I had had quite enough of the place that had enchanted me up to the last four-and-twenty hours. I began to see myself back in Elm Park Gardens. There, at least, if also there alone, I should get some credit for what I had done.

It was no use looking for Bob upon the terrace now; yet I did look there, among other obvious places, before I could bring myself to knock at his door. There was a light in his room, so I knew that he was there, and he cried out admittance in so sharp a tone that I fancied he also knew who knocked. I found him packing in his shirt-sleeves. He received me with a stare in exact keeping with his tone. What on earth had Mrs. Lascelles said?

"Going away?" I asked, as a mere preliminary, and I shut the door behind me. Bob followed the action with raised eyebrows, then flung me the shortest possible affirmative, as he bent once more over the suit-case on the bed.

But in a few seconds he looked up.

"Anything I can do for you, Clephane?"

"That depends where you are going."

Bob went on packing with a smile. I guessed where he was going. "I thought there might be something pressing," he remarked, without looking up again.

"There is," said I. "There is something you can do for me on the spot. You can try to believe that I have not meant to be quite such a skunk as I may have seemed—to you," I was on the point of adding, but I stopped short of that advisedly, as I thought of Mrs. Lascelles also.

"Oh, that's all right," said Bob, in a would-be airy tone that carried its own contradiction. "All's fair, according to the proverb; I no more blame you than you would have blamed me. I hope, on the contrary, that I may congratulate you."

And he stood up with a look which, coupled with his words, made it my turn to stare.

"Indeed you may not," said I.

"Aren't you engaged to her?" he asked.

"Good God, no!" I cried. "What made you think so?"

"Everything!" exclaimed Bob, after a moment's pause of obvious bewilderment. "I—you see—I had a note from Mrs. Lascelles herself!"

"Yes?" said I, carefully careless, but I wanted more than ever to know that missive's gist.

"Only a few lines," Bob went on, ruefully; "they are the first thing I heard or saw when I got down, and they almost made me wish I'd come down with a run! Well, it's no use talking about it, I only thought you'd know. It was the usual smack in the eye, I suppose, only nicely put and all that. She didn't tell me where she was going, or why; she told me I had better ask you."

"But you wouldn't condescend."

Bob gave a rather friendly little laugh.

"I said I'd see you damned!" he admitted. "But of course I thought you were the lucky man. I still half believe you are!"

"Well, I'm not."

"Do you mean to say that she's refused you too?"

"She hasn't had the chance."

Bob's eyes opened to an infantile width.

"But you told me you were in earnest!" he urged.

"As much in earnest as you were, I believe was what I said."

"That's the same thing," returned Bob, sharply. "You may not think it is. I don't care what you think. But I'm very sorry you said you were in earnest if you were not."

And his tone convinced me that he was no longer commiserating himself; he was sorry on some new account, and the evident reality of his regret filled me in turn with all the qualms of a guilty conscience.

"Why are you sorry?" I demanded.

"Oh, not on my own account," said Bob. "I'm delighted, personally, of course."

"Then do you mean to say—you actually told her—I was as much in earnest as you were?"

Bob Evers smiled openly in my face; it was the only revenge he ever took; and even it was tempered by the inextinguishable sweetness of expression and the childlike wide-eyed candour which were Bob's even in the hour of his humiliation, and will be, one hopes, all his days.

"Not in so many words," he said, "but I am afraid I did tell her in effect. You see, I took you at your word. I thought it was quite true. I'm awfully sorry, Duncan. But it really does serve you right!"

I made no answer. I was looking at the suit-case on the bed. Bob seemed to have lost all interest in his packing. I turned to leave him without a word.

"I am awfully sorry!" he was the one to say again. I began to wonder when he would see all round the point, and how it would affect his feeling (to say nothing of his actions) when he did. Meanwhile it was Bob who was holding out his hand.

"So am I," I said, taking it.

And for once I, too, was not thinking about myself.

CHAPTER XII

A STERN CHASE

Where had Bob been going, and where was he going now? If these were not the first questions that I asked myself on coming away from him, they were at all events among my last thoughts that night, and as it happened, quite my first next morning. His voice had reached me through my bedroom window, on the head of a dream about himself. I got up and looked out; there was Bob Evers seeing the suit-case into the tiny train which brings your baggage (and yourself, if you like) to the very door of the Riffel Alp Hotel. Bob did not like and I watched him out of sight down the winding path threaded by the shining rails. He walked slowly, head and shoulders bent, it might be with dogged resolve, it might be in mere depression; there was never a glimpse of his face, nor a backward glance as he swung round the final corner, with his great-coat over his arm.

In spite of my curiosity as to his destination, I made no attempt to discover it for myself, but on consideration I was guilty of certain inquiries concerning that of Mrs. Lascelles. They had not to be very exhaustive; she had made no secret of her original plans upon leaving the Riffel Alp, and they did not appear to have undergone much change. I myself left the same forenoon, and lay that night amid the smells of

E. W. Hornung

Brigues, after a little tour of its hotels, in one of which I found the name of Mrs. Lascelles in the register, while in every one I was prepared to light upon Bob Evers in the flesh. But that encounter did not occur.

In the early morning I was one of a shivering handful who awaited the diligence for the Furka Pass; and an ominous drizzle made me thankful that my telegram of the previous day had been too late to secure me an outside seat. It was quite damp enough within. Nor did the day improve as we drove, or the view attract me in the least. It was at its worst as a sight, and I at mine as a sightseer. I have as little recollection of my fellow-passengers; but I still see the page in the hotel register at the Rhone Glacier, with the name I sought written boldly in its place, just twenty-four hours earlier.

The Furka Pass has its European reputation; it would gain nothing from my enthusiastic praises, had I any enthusiasm to draw upon, or the descriptive powers to do it justice. But what I best remember is the time it took us to climb those interminable zig-zags, and to shake off the too tenacious sight of the hotel in the hollow where I had seen a signature and eaten my lunch. Now I think of it, there were two couples who had come so far with us, but at the Rhone Glacier they exchanged their mutually demonstrative adieux, and I thought the couple who came on would never have done waving to the couple who stayed behind. They kept it up for at least an hour, and then broke out again at each of our many last glimpses of the hotel, now hundreds of feet below. That was the only diversion until these energetic people went to see the glacier cave at the summit of the pass. I am glad to remember that I preferred refreshment at the inn. After that, night fell upon a scene whose desolation impressed me more than its grandeur, and so in the end we rattled into Andermatt: here was a huge hotel all but empty, with a perfect tome of a visitors' book, and in it sure enough the fine free autograph which I was beginning to know so well.

"Yes, sare," said the concierge, "the season end suddenly mit the bad vedder at the beginning of the veek. You know that lady? She has been here last night; she go avay again to-day, on to Goeschenen and Zuerich. Yes, sare, she shall be in Zuerich to-night."

I was in Zuerich myself the night after. I knew the hotel to go to, knew it from Mrs. Lascelles herself, whose experience of continental hotels was so pathetically extensive. This was the best in Switzerland, so she had assured me in one of our talks: she could never pass through Zuerich without making a night of it at the Baur au Lac. But one night of it appeared to be enough, or so it had proved on this occasion, for again I missed her by a few hours. I was annoyed. I agreed with Mrs. Lascelles about this hotel. Since I had made up my mind to overtake her first or last, it might as well have been a comfortable place like this, where there was good cooking and good music and all the comforts which I may or may not have needed, but which I was certainly beginning to desire.

What a contrast to the place at which I found myself the following night. It was a place called Triberg, in the Black Forest, which I had never penetrated before, and certainly never shall again. It seemed to me an uttermost end of the earth, but it was raining when I arrived, and the rain never ceased for an instant while I was there. About a dozen hotel omnibuses met the train, from which only three passengers alighted; the other two were a young married couple at whom I would not have looked twice, though we all boarded the same lucky 'bus, had not the young man stared very hard at me.

E. W. Hornung

"Captain Clephane," said he, "I guess you've forgotten me; but you may remember my best gurl?"

It was our good-natured young American from the Riffel Alp, who had not only joined in the daily laugh against himself up there, but must needs raise it as soon as ever he met one of us again. I rather think his best girl did not hear him, for she was staring through the streaming omnibus windows into an absolutely deserted country street, and I feared that her eyes would soon resemble the panes. She brightened, however, in a very flattering way, as I thought, on finding a third soul for one or both of them to speak to, for a change. I only wished I could have returned the compliment in my heart.

"Captain Clephane," continued the young bridegroom, "we came down Monday last. Say, who do you guess came down along with us?"

"A friend of yours," prompted the bride, as I put on as blank an expression as possible.

I opened my eyes a little wider. It seemed the only thing to do.

"Captain Clephane," said the bridegroom, beaming all over his good-humoured face, "it was a lady named Lascelles, and it's to her advice we owe this pleasure. We travelled together as far as Loocerne. We guess we'll put salt on her at this hotel."

"So does the Captain," announced the bride, who could not look at me without a smile, which I altogether declined to return. But I need hardly confess that she was right. It was from Mrs. Lascelles that I also had heard of the dismal spot to which we were come, as her own ultimate objective after

Switzerland. It was the only address with which she had provided the concierge at the Riffel Alp. All day I had regretted the night wasted at Zuerich, on the chance of saving a day; but until this moment I had been sanguine of bringing my dubious quest to a successful issue here in Triberg. Now I was no longer even anxious to do so. I did not desire witnesses of a meeting which might well be of a character humiliating to myself. Still less should I have chosen for such witnesses a couple who were plainly disposed to put the usual misconstruction upon the relations of any man with any woman.

My disappointment was consequently less than theirs when we drove up to as gloomy a hostelry as I have ever beheld, with the blue-black forest smoking wet behind it, to find that here also the foul weather had brought the season to a premature and sudden end, literally emptying this particular hotel. Nor did the landlord give us the welcome we might have expected on a hasty consideration of the circumstances. He said that he had been on the point of shutting up that house until next season and hinted at less profit than loss upon three persons only.

"But there's a fourth person coming," declared the disconsolate bride. "We figured on finding her right here!"

"A Mrs. Lascelles," her husband explained.

"Been and gone," said the landlord, grinning sardonically. "Too lonely for the lady. She has arrived last night, and gone away again this morning. You will find her at the Darmstaedterhof, in Baden-Baden, unless she changes her mind on the way."

I caught his grin. It had been the same story, at every stage of my journey; the chances were that it would be the same thing

E. W. Hornung

again at Baden-Baden. There may have been something, however, of which I was unaware in my smile; for I found myself under close observation by the bride; and as our eyes met her hand slipped within her husband's arm.

"I guess *we* won't find her there," she said. "I guess we'll just light out for ourselves, and wish the captain luck."

A stern chase is proverbially protracted, but on dry land it has usually one end. Mine ended in Baden on the fifth (and first fine) day, rather early in the afternoon. On arrival I drove straight to the Darmstaedterhof, and asked to see no visitors' books, for the five days had taken the edge off my finesse, but inquired at once whether a Mrs. Lascelles was staying there or not. She was. It seemed incredible. Were they sure she had not just left? They were sure. But she was not in; at my request they made equally sure of that. She had probably gone to the Conversationshaus, to listen to the band. All Baden went there in the afternoon, to listen to that band. It was a very good band. Baden-Baden was a very good place. There was no better hotel in Baden-Baden than the Darmstaedterhof; there were no such baths in the other hotels, these came straight from the spring, at their natural temperature. They were matchless for rheumatism, especially in the legs. The old Empress, Augusta, when in Baden, used to patronise this very hotel and no other. They could show me the actual bath, and I myself could have pension (baths excluded) for eight marks and fifty a day. If I would be so kind as to step into the lift, I should see the room for myself, and then with my permission they would bring in my luggage and pay the cab.

All this by degrees, from a pale youth in frock-coat and forage-cap, and a more prosperous personage with *pince-nez* and a paunch (yet another concierge and my latest landlord respectively), while I stood making up my mind. The closing proposition was of some assistance to me. I had no luggage on the cab, of which the cabman's hat alone was visible, at the bottom of a flight of steps, at the far end of the flagged approach. I had left my luggage at the station, but I only recollected the fact upon being recalled from a mental forecast of the interview before me to these exceedingly petty preliminaries.

There and then I paid off the cab and found my own way to this Conversationshaus. I liked the look of the trim, fresh town in its perfect amphitheatre of pine-clad hills, covered in by a rich blue sky from which the last clouds were exhaling like breath from a mirror. The well-drained streets were drying clean as in a black frost; checkered with sharp shadows, twinkling with shop windows, and strikingly free from the more cumbrous forms of traffic. If this was Germany, I could dispense with certain discreditable prejudices. I had to inquire my way of a policeman in a flaming helm; because I could not understand his copious directions, he led me to a tiny bridge within earshot of the band, and there refused my proferred coin with the dignity of a Hohenzollern. Under the tiny bridge there ran the shallowest and clearest of little rivers. Up the white walls of the houses clambered a deal of Virginia creeper, brought on by the rain, and now almost scarlet in the strong sunlight. Presently at some gates there was a mark to pay, or it may have been two; immediate admittance to an avenue of fascinating shops, with an inner avenue of trees, little tables under them, and the crash of the band growing louder at every yard. Eventual access to a fine, broad terrace, a fine, long facade, a bandstand, and people listening and walking up and down, people listening and drinking beer or coffee at more little tables, people listening and reading on rows of chairs, people standing to listen with all their ears; but not for a long time the person I sought.

E. W. Hornung

* * * * *

Not for a very long time, but yet, at last, and all alone, among the readers on the chairs, deep in a Tauchnitz volume even here as in the Alps; more daintily yet not less simply dressed, in pink muslin and a big black hat; and blessed here as there with such blooming health, such inimitable freshness, such a general air of well-being and of deep content, as almost to disgust me after my whole week's search and my own hourly qualms.

So I found Mrs. Lascelles in the end, and so I saw her until she looked up and saw me; then the picture changed; but I am not going to describe the change.

"Well, really!" she cried out.

"It has taken me all the week to find you," said I, as I replaced my hat.

Her eyes flashed again.

"Has it, indeed! And now you have found me, aren't you satisfied? Pray have a good look, Captain Clephane. You won't find anybody else!"

Her meaning dawned on me at last.

"I didn't expect to, Mrs. Lascelles."

"Am I to believe that?"

"You must do as you please. It is the truth. Mrs. Lascelles, I have been all the week looking for you and you alone."

I spoke with some warmth, for not only did I speak the truth, but it had become more and more the truth at every stage of my journey since Brigues. Mrs. Lascelles leant back in her chair and surveyed me with less anger, but with the purer and more pernicious scorn.

"And what business had you to do that?" she asked calmly. "How dare you, I should like to know?"

"I dared," said I, "because I owed you a debt which, I felt, must be paid in person, or it would never be paid at all. Mrs. Lascelles, I owed and do owe you about the most abject apology man ever made! I have followed you all this way for no other earthly reason than to make it, in all sincere humility. But it has taken me more or less since Tuesday morning; and I can't kneel here. Do you mind if I sit down?"

Mrs. Lascelles drew in the hem of her pink muslin, with an all but insufferable gesture of unwilling resignation. I took the next chair but one, but, leaning my elbow on the chair-back between us, was rather the gainer by the intervening inches, which enabled me to study a perfect profile and the most wonderful colouring as I could scarcely have done at still closer range. She never turned to look at me, but simply listened while the band played, and people passed, and I said my say. It was very short: there was so little that she did not know. There was the excitement about Bob, his subsequent reappearance, our scene in his room and my last sight of him in the morning; but the bare facts went into few words, and there was no demand for details. Mrs. Lascelles seemed to have lost all interest in her latest lover; but when I tried to speak of my own hateful hand in that affair, to explain what I could of it, but to extenuate nothing, and to apologise from my heart for it all, then there was a change in her, then her blood mounted, then her bosom heaved, and I was silenced by a single flash from her eyes.

"Yes," said she, "you could let him think you were in earnest, you could pose as his rival, you could pretend all that! Not to me, I grant you! Even you did not go quite so far as that; or was it that you knew that I should see through you? You made up for it, however, the other night. That I never, never, never shall forgive. I, who had never seriously thought of accepting him, who was only hesitating in order to refuse him in the most deliberate and final manner imaginable—I, to have the word put into my mouth—by you! I, who was going in any case, of my own accord, to be told to go—by you! One thing you will never know, Captain Clephane, and that is how nearly you drove me into marrying him just to spite you and his miserable mother. I meant to do it, that night when I left you. It would have served you right if I had!"

She did not rise. She did not look at me again. But I saw the tears standing in her eyes, one I saw roll down her cheek, and the sight smote me harder than her hardest word, though more words followed in broken whispers.

"It wasn't because I cared ... that you hurt me as you did. I never did care for him ... like that. It was ... because ... you seemed to think my society contamination ... to an honest boy. I did care for him, but not like that. I cared too much for him to let him marry me ... to contaminate him for life!"

I repudiated the reiterated word with all my might. I had never used it, even in my thoughts; it had never once occurred to me in connection with her. Had I not shown as much? Had I behaved as though I feared contamination for myself? I rapped out these questions with undue triumph, in my heat, only to perceive their second edge as it cut me to the quick.

"But you were playing a part," retorted Mrs. Lascelles. "You don't deny it. Are you proud of it, that you rub it in? Or are you going to begin denying it now?"

Unfortunately, that was impossible. Tt was too late for denials. But, driven into my last corner, as it seemed, I relapsed for the moment into thought, and my thoughts took the form of a rapid retrospect of all the hours that this angry woman and I had spent together. I was introduced to her again by poor Bob. I recognised her again by the light of a match, and accosted her next morning in the strong sunshine. We went for our first walk together. We sat together on the green ledge overlooking the glaciers, and first she talked about herself, and then we both talked about Bob, and then Bob appeared in the flesh and gave me my disastrous idea. Then there was the day on the Findelen that we had all three spent together. Then there was the walk home from early church (short as it had been), the subsequent expedition to Zermatt and back, with its bright beginning and its clouded end. Up to that point, at all events, they had been happy hours, so many of them unburdened by a single thought of Bob Evers and his folly, not one of them haunted by the usual sense of a part that is played. I almost wondered as I realised this. I supposed it would be no use attempting to express myself to Mrs. Lascelles, but I felt I must say something before I went, so I said:

"I deny nothing, and I'm proud of nothing, but neither am I quite so ashamed as perhaps I ought to be. Shall I tell you why, Mrs. Lascelles? It may have been an insolent and an infamous part, as you imply; but I enjoyed playing it, and I used often to forget it was a part at all. So much so that even now I'm not so sure that it was one! There—I suppose that makes it all ten times worse. But I won't apologise again. Do you mind giving me that stick?"

I had rested the two of them against the chair between us.

E. W. Hornung

Mrs. Lascelles had taken possession of one, with which she was methodically probing the path, for there had been no time to draw their Alpine teeth. She did not comply with my request. She smiled instead.

"I mind very much," her old voice said. "Now we have finished fighting, perhaps you will listen to the *Meistersinger* —for it is worth listening to on that band—and try to appreciate Baden while you are here. There are no more trains for hours."

The wooded hills rose over the bandstand, against the bright blue sky. The shadow of the colonnade lay sharp and black beyond our feet, with people passing, and the band crashing, in the sunlight beyond. That was Baden. I should not have found it a difficult place to appreciate, a week or so before; even now it was no hardship to sit there listening to the one bit of Wagner that my ear welcomes as a friend, and furtively to watch my companion as she sat and listened too. You will perceive by what train of associations my eyes soon fell upon the Tauchnitz volume which she must have placed without thinking on the chair between us. I took it up. Heavens! It was one of the volumes of Browning's Poems. And back I sped in spirit to a green ledge overlooking the Gorner Glacier, to think what we had said about Browning up there, but only to remember how I had longed to be to Mrs. Lascelles what Catherine Evers had been to me. There were some sharp edges to the reminiscence, but I turned the pages while they did their worst, and so cut myself to the heart upon a sharper than them all. It was in a poem I remembered, a poem whose title pained me into glancing farther. And see what leapt to meet me from the printed page:

"And I,—what I seem to my friend, you see: What I soon shall seem to his love, you guess: What I seem to myself, do you ask of me?   No hero, I confess."

True, too true; no hero, indeed; anything in the wide world else! But that I should read it there by the woman's side! And yet, even that was no such coincidence; had we not talked about the poet, had I not implied what Catherine thought of him, what everybody ought to think?

Of a sudden a strange thrill stirred me; sidelong I glanced at my companion. She had turned her head away; her cheek was deeply dyed. She knew what I was doing; she might divine my thoughts. I shut the book lest she should see the vile title of a thing I had hitherto liked. And the *Prizelied* crashed back into the ear.

CHAPTER XIII

NUMBER THREE

It was the middle of November when I was shown once more into the old room at the old number in Elm Park Gardens. There was a fire, the windows were shut, and the electric light was a distinct improvement when the maid put it on; otherwise all was exactly as I had left it in August, and so often pictured it since. There was "Hope," presiding over the shelf of poets, and here "Paolo and Francesca," reminiscent as ever of Melbury Road, upon a wet Sunday, years and years ago. The day's *Times* and the week's *Spectator* were not less prominent than the last new problem novel; all three lay precisely where their predecessors had always lain; and my own dead self stood in its own old place upon the piano which had been in St. Helena with Napoleon. It is vanity's deserts to come across these unnecessary memorials of a decently buried boyhood; there is always something stultifying about them, and I longed to confiscate this one of me.

But there was a photograph on the chimney-piece that interested me keenly; it was evidently the very latest of Bob Evers, and I studied it with a painful curiosity. Was the boy really altered, or did I only imagine it from my secret knowledge of his affairs? To me he seemed graver, more sedate, less angelically trustful in expression, and yet something finer and manlier withal: to confirm the idea one had only to compare this new one with the racket photograph now relegated to a rear rank. The round-eyed look was gone. Had I here yet another memorial of yet another buried boyhood? If so, I felt I was the sexton, and I might be ashamed, and I was.

"Looking at Bob? Isn't it a dear one of him? You see—he is none the worse!"

And Catherine Evers stood smiling as warmly, as gratefully, as she grasped my hand; but with her warmth there was a certain nervousness of manner, which had the odd effect of putting me perversely at my ease; and I found myself looking critically at Catherine, really critically, for I suppose the first time in my life.

"He is playing foot-ball," she continued, full as ever of her boy. "I had a letter from him only this morning. He had his colours at Eton, you know (he had them for everything there), but he never dreamt of getting them at Cambridge, yet now he really thinks he has a chance! They tried him the other day, and he kicked a goal. Dear old Bob! If he does get them he will be a Blue and a half, he says. He writes so happily, Duncan! I have so much to be thankful for—to thank you for!"

Yes, Catherine was good to look at; there was no doubt of it; and this time she was not wearing any hat. Discoursing of the lad, she was animated, eager, for once as exclamatory as her pen, with light and life in every look of the thin intellectual face, in every glance of the large, intellectual eyes, and in every intonation of the keen dry voice. A sweet woman; a young woman; a woman with a full heart of love and sympathy and tenderness—for Bob! Yet, when she thanked me at the end, either upon an impulse, or because she thought she must, her eyes fell, and again I detected that slight embarrassment which was none the less a revelation, to me, in Catherine Evers, of all women in the world.

"We won't speak of that," I said, "if you don't mind. I am not proud of it."

Catherine scanned me more narrowly. I knew her better with that look. "Then tell me about yourself, and do sit down," she said, drawing a chair near the fire, but sitting on the other side of it herself. "I needn't ask you how you are. I never saw you looking so well. That comes of going right away and not hurrying back. I think you were so wise! But, Duncan, I am sorry to see both sticks still! Have you seen your man since you came back?"

"I have."

"Well?"

"I'm afraid there's no more soldiering for me."

Catherine seemed more than sorry and disappointed; she looked quite indignant with the eminent specialist who had finally pronounced this opinion. Was I sure he was the very best man for that kind of thing? She would have a second opinion, if she were me. Very well, then, a third and fourth! If there was one man she pitied from the bottom of her heart, it was the man without a profession or an occupation of some kind. Catherine looked, however, as though her pity were almost akin to horror.

"I have a trifle, luckily," I said. "I must try something else."

Catherine stared into the fire, as though thinking of

something else for me to try. She seemed full of apprehension on my account.

"Don't you worry about me," I went on. "I came here to talk
about somebody else, of course."

Catherine almost started.

"I've told you about Bob," she said, with a suspicious upward
glance from the fire.

"I don't mean Bob," said I, "or anything you may think I did
for him or you. I said just now that I didn't want to speak of
it and no more I do. Yet, as a matter of fact, I do want to
speak to you about the lady in that case."

Catherine's face betrayed the mixed emotions of relief and
fresh alarm.

"You don't mean to say the creature—? But it's impossible. I
heard from Bob only this morning. He wrote so happily!"

I could not help smiling at the nature and quality of the
alarm.

"They have seen nothing more of each other, if that's what
you fear," said I. "But what I do want to speak about is this
creature, as you call her, and no one else. She has done
nothing to deserve quite so much contempt. I want you to be
just to her, Catherine."

I was serious. I may have been ridiculous. Catherine evidently found me so, for, after gauging me with that wry but
humourous look which I knew so well of old, for which I had
been waiting this afternoon, she went off into the decorous
little fit of laughter in which it had invariably ended.

"Forgive me, Duncan dear! But you do look so serious, and you *are* so dreadfully broad! I never was. I hope you remember that? Broad minds and easy principles—the combination is inevitable. But, really though, Duncan, is there anything to be said for her? Was she a possible person, in any sense of the word?"

"Quite a probable person," I assured Catherine.

"But I have heard all sorts of things about her!"

"From Bob?"

"No, he never mentioned her."

"Nor me, perhaps?"

"Nor you, Duncan. I am afraid there may be just a drop of bad blood there! You see, he looked upon you as a successful rival. You wrote and told me so, if you remember, from some place on your way down from the mountains. Your letter and Bob arrived the same night."

I nodded.

"It was so clever of you!" pursued Catherine. "Quite brilliant; but I don't quite know what to say to your letting my baby climb that awful Matterhorn; in a fog, too!"

And there was real though momentary reproach in the firelit face.

"I couldn't very well stop him, you know. Besides," I added, "it was such a chance."

"Of what?"

"Of getting rid of Mrs. Lascelles. I thought you would think it worth the risk."

"I do," declared Catherine, on due consultation with the fire. "I really do! Bob is all I have—all I want—in this world, Duncan; and it may seem a dreadful thing to say, and you mayn't believe it when I've said it, but—yes!—I'd rather he had never come home at all than come home married, at his age, and to an Indian widow, whose first husband had divorced her! I mean it, Duncan; I do indeed!"

"I am sure you do," said I. "It was just what I said to myself."

"To think of my Bob being Number Three!" murmured Catherine, with that plaintive drollery of hers which I had found irresistible in the days of old.

I was able to resist it now. "So those were the things you heard?" I remarked.

"Yes," said Catherine; "haven't you heard them?"

"I didn't need. I knew her in India years ago."

Catherine's eyes opened.

"*you* knew this Mrs. Lascelles?"

"Before that was her name. I have also met her original husband. If you had known him, you would be less hard on her."

Catherine's eyes were still wide open. They were rather hard eyes, after all. "Why did you not tell me you had known her, when you wrote?" she asked.

E. W. Hornung

"It wouldn't have done any good. I did what you wanted done, you know. I thought that was enough."

"It was enough," echoed Catherine, with a quick return of grace. She looked into the fire. "I don't want to be hard upon the poor thing, Duncan! I know you think we women always are, upon each other. But to have come back married—at his age—to even the nicest woman in the world! It would have been madness ... ruination ... Duncan, I'm going to say something else that may shock you."

"Say away," said I.

Her voice had fallen. She was looking at me very narrowly, as if to measure the effect of her unspoken words.

"I am not so very sure about marriage," she went on, "at any age! Don't misunderstand me ... I was very happy ... but I for one could never marry again ... and I am not sure that I ever want to see Bob...."

Catherine had spoken very gently, looking once more in the fire; when she ceased there was a space of utter silence in the little room. Then her eyes came back furtively to mine; and presently they were twinkling with their old staid merriment.

"But to be Number Three!" she said again. "My poor old Bob!"

And she smiled upon me, tenderly, from the depths of her alter-egoism.

"Well," I said, "he never will be."

"God forbid!" cried Catherine.

"He has forbidden. It will never happen."

"Is she dead?" asked Catherine, but not too quickly for common decency. She was not one to pass such bounds.

"Not that I know of."

It was hard to repress a sneer.

"Then what makes you so sure—that he never could?"

"Well, he never will in my time!"

"You are good to me," said Catherine, gratefully.

"Not a bit good," said I, "or—only to myself ... I have been good to no one else in this whole matter. That's what it all amounts to, and that's what I really came to tell you. Catherine ... I am married to her myself!"

THE END

E. W. Hornung

ABOUT THE AUTHOR

Ernest William Hornung (June 7, 1866 – March 22, 1921) was a British author.

Hornung was the third son of John Peter Hornung, a Hungarian, and was born in Middlesbrough. He was educated at Uppingham during some of the later years of its great headmaster, Edward Thring. He spent most of his life in England and France, but in 1884 left for Australia and stayed for two years where he working as a tutor at Mossgiel station. Although his Australian experience had been so short, it coloured most of his literary work from A Bride from the Bush published in 1899, to Old Offenders and a few Old Scores, which appeared after his death.

After he returned from Australia in 1886, he married Constance Doyle, the sister of Sir Arthur Conan Doyle in 1893. Hornung published the poems Bond and Free and Wooden Crosses in The Times. The character of A. J. Raffles, a "gentleman thief", first appeared in Strand Magazine and then in other British magazines during the 1890s. The stories were later published in The Amateur Cracksman (1899), a collection. Other titles in the series include The Black Mask (1901), A Thief in the Night (1905), and the full-length novel Mr. Justice Raffles (1909).

Choose from Thousands of 1stWorldLibrary Classics By

A. M. Barnard	Booth Tarkington	Edward Everett Hale
Ada Leverson	Boyd Cable	Edward J. O'Biren
Adolphus William Ward	Bram Stoker	Edward S. Ellis
Aesop	C. Collodi	Edwin L. Arnold
Agatha Christie	C. E. Orr	Eleanor Atkins
Alexander Aaronsohn	C. M. Ingleby	Eleanor Hallowell Abbott
Alexander Kielland	Carolyn Wells	Eliot Gregory
Alexandre Dumas	Catherine Parr Traill	Elizabeth Gaskell
Alfred Gatty	Charles A. Eastman	Elizabeth McCracken
Alfred Ollivant	Charles Amory Beach	Elizabeth Von Arnim
Alice Duer Miller	Charles Dickens	Ellem Key
Alice Turner Curtis	Charles Dudley Warner	Emerson Hough
Alice Dunbar	Charles Farrar Browne	Emilie F. Carlen
Allen Chapman	Charles Ives	Emily Bronte
Alleyne Ireland	Charles Kingsley	Emily Dickinson
Ambrose Bierce	Charles Klein	Enid Bagnold
Amelia E. Barr	Charles Hanson Towne	Enilor Macartney Lane
Amory H. Bradford	Charles Lathrop Pack	Erasmus W. Jones
Andrew Lang	Charles Romyn Dake	Ernie Howard Pie
Andrew McFarland Davis	Charles Whibley	Ethel May Dell
Andy Adams	Charles Willing Beale	Ethel Turner
Angela Brazil	Charlotte M. Braeme	Ethel Watts Mumford
Anna Alice Chapin	Charlotte M. Yonge	Eugene Sue
Anna Sewell	Charlotte Perkins Stetson	Eugenie Foa
Annie Besant	Clair W. Hayes	Eugene Wood
Annie Hamilton Donnell	Clarence Day Jr.	Eustace Hale Ball
Annie Payson Call	Clarence E. Mulford	Evelyn Everett-green
Annie Roe Carr	Clemence Housman	Everard Cotes
Annonaymous	Confucius	F. H. Cheley
Anton Chekhov	Coningsby Dawson	F. J. Cross
Archibald Lee Fletcher	Cornelis DeWitt Wilcox	F. Marion Crawford
Arnold Bennett	Cyril Burleigh	Fannie E. Newberry
Arthur C. Benson	D. H. Lawrence	Federick Austin Ogg
Arthur Conan Doyle	Daniel Defoe	Ferdinand Ossendowski
Arthur M. Winfield	David Garnett	Fergus Hume
Arthur Ransome	Dinah Craik	Florence A. Kilpatrick
Arthur Schnitzler	Don Carlos Janes	Fremont B. Deering
Arthur Train	Donald Keyhoe	Francis Bacon
Atticus	Dorothy Kilner	Francis Darwin
B.H. Baden-Powell	Dougan Clark	Frances Hodgson Burnett
B. M. Bower	Douglas Fairbanks	Frances Parkinson Keyes
B. C. Chatterjee	E. Nesbit	Frank Gee Patchin
Baroness Emmuska Orczy	E. P. Roe	Frank Harris
Baroness Orczy	E. Phillips Oppenheim	Frank Jewett Mather
Basil King	E. S. Brooks	Frank L. Packard
Bayard Taylor	Earl Barnes	Frank V. Webster
Ben Macomber	Edgar Rice Burroughs	Frederic Stewart Isham
Bertha Muzzy Bower	Edith Van Dyne	Frederick Trevor Hill
Bjornstjerne Bjornson	Edith Wharton	Frederick Winslow Taylor

Friedrich Kerst
Friedrich Nietzsche
Fyodor Dostoyevsky
G.A. Henty
G.K. Chesterton
Gabrielle E. Jackson
Garrett P. Serviss
Gaston Leroux
George A. Warren
George Ade
Geroge Bernard Shaw
George Cary Eggleston
George Durston
George Ebers
George Eliot
George Gissing
George MacDonald
George Meredith
George Orwell
George Sylvester Viereck
George Tucker
George W. Cable
George Wharton James
Gertrude Atherton
Gordon Casserly
Grace E. King
Grace Gallatin
Grace Greenwood
Grant Allen
Guillermo A. Sherwell
Gulielma Zollinger
Gustav Flaubert
H. A. Cody
H. B. Irving
H.C. Bailey
H. G. Wells
H. H. Munro
H. Irving Hancock
H. R. Naylor
H. Rider Haggard
H. W. C. Davis
Haldeman Julius
Hall Caine
Hamilton Wright Mabie
Hans Christian Andersen
Harold Avery
Harold McGrath
Harriet Beecher Stowe
Harry Castlemon
Harry Coghill
Harry Houidini

Hayden Carruth
Helent Hunt Jackson
Helen Nicolay
Hendrik Conscience
Hendy David Thoreau
Henri Barbusse
Henrik Ibsen
Henry Adams
Henry Ford
Henry Frost
Henry James
Henry Jones Ford
Henry Seton Merriman
Henry W Longfellow
Herbert A. Giles
Herbert Carter
Herbert N. Casson
Herman Hesse
Hildegard G. Frey
Homer
Honore De Balzac
Horace B. Day
Horace Walpole
Horatio Alger Jr.
Howard Pyle
Howard R. Garis
Hugh Lofting
Hugh Walpole
Humphry Ward
Ian Maclaren
Inez Haynes Gillmore
Irving Bacheller
Isabel Cecilia Williams
Isabel Hornibrook
Israel Abrahams
Ivan Turgenev
J.G.Austin
J. Henri Fabre
J. M. Barrie
J. M. Walsh
J. Macdonald Oxley
J. R. Miller
J. S. Fletcher
J. S. Knowles
J. Storer Clouston
J. W. Duffield
Jack London
Jacob Abbott
James Allen
James Andrews
James Baldwin

James Branch Cabell
James DeMille
James Joyce
James Lane Allen
James Lane Allen
James Oliver Curwood
James Oppenheim
James Otis
James R. Driscoll
Jane Abbott
Jane Austen
Jane L. Stewart
Janet Aldridge
Jens Peter Jacobsen
Jerome K. Jerome
Jessie Graham Flower
John Buchan
John Burroughs
John Cournos
John F. Kennedy
John Gay
John Glasworthy
John Habberton
John Joy Bell
John Kendrick Bangs
John Milton
John Philip Sousa
John Taintor Foote
Jonas Lauritz Idemil Lie
Jonathan Swift
Joseph A. Altsheler
Joseph Carey
Joseph Conrad
Joseph E. Badger Jr
Joseph Hergesheimer
Joseph Jacobs
Jules Vernes
Julian Hawthrone
Julie A Lippmann
Justin Huntly McCarthy
Kakuzo Okakura
Karle Wilson Baker
Kate Chopin
Kenneth Grahame
Kenneth McGaffey
Kate Langley Bosher
Kate Langley Bosher
Katherine Cecil Thurston
Katherine Stokes
L. A. Abbot
L. T. Meade

L. Frank Baum
Latta Griswold
Laura Dent Crane
Laura Lee Hope
Laurence Housman
Lawrence Beasley
Leo Tolstoy
Leonid Andreyev
Lewis Carroll
Lewis Sperry Chafer
Lilian Bell
Lloyd Osbourne
Louis Hughes
Louis Joseph Vance
Louis Tracy
Louisa May Alcott
Lucy Fitch Perkins
Lucy Maud Montgomery
Luther Benson
Lydia Miller Middleton
Lyndon Orr
M. Corvus
M. H. Adams
Margaret E. Sangster
Margret Howth
Margaret Vandercook
Margaret W. Hungerford
Margret Penrose
Maria Edgeworth
Maria Thompson Daviess
Mariano Azuela
Marion Polk Angellotti
Mark Overton
Mark Twain
Mary Austin
Mary Catherine Crowley
Mary Cole
Mary Hastings Bradley
Mary Roberts Rinehart
Mary Rowlandson
M. Wollstonecraft Shelley
Maud Lindsay
Max Beerbohm
Myra Kelly
Nathaniel Hawthrone
Nicolo Machiavelli
O. F. Walton
Oscar Wilde

Owen Johnson
P.G. Wodehouse
Paul and Mabel Thorne
Paul G. Tomlinson
Paul Severing
Percy Brebner
Percy Keese Fitzhugh
Peter B. Kyne
Plato
Quincy Allen
R. Derby Holmes
R. L. Stevenson
R. S. Ball
Rabindranath Tagore
Rahul Alvares
Ralph Bonehill
Ralph Henry Barbour
Ralph Victor
Ralph Waldo Emmerson
Rene Descartes
Ray Cummings
Rex Beach
Rex E. Beach
Richard Harding Davis
Richard Jefferies
Richard Le Gallienne
Robert Barr
Robert Frost
Robert Gordon Anderson
Robert L. Drake
Robert Lansing
Robert Lynd
Robert Michael Ballantyne
Robert W. Chambers
Rosa Nouchette Carey
Rudyard Kipling
Saint Augustine
Samuel B. Allison
Samuel Hopkins Adams
Sarah Bernhardt
Sarah C. Hallowell
Selma Lagerlof
Sherwood Anderson
Sigmund Freud
Standish O'Grady
Stanley Weyman
Stella Benson
Stella M. Francis

Stephen Crane
Stewart Edward White
Stijn Streuvels
Swami Abhedananda
Swami Parmananda
T. S. Ackland
T. S. Arthur
The Princess Der Ling
Thomas A. Janvier
Thomas A Kempis
Thomas Anderton
Thomas Bailey Aldrich
Thomas Bulfinch
Thomas De Quincey
Thomas Dixon
Thomas H. Huxley
Thomas Hardy
Thomas More
Thornton W. Burgess
U. S. Grant
Upton Sinclair
Valentine Williams
Various Authors
Vaughan Kester
Victor Appleton
Victor G. Durham
Victoria Cross
Virginia Woolf
Wadsworth Camp
Walter Camp
Walter Scott
Washington Irving
Wilbur Lawton
Wilkie Collins
Willa Cather
Willard F. Baker
William Dean Howells
William le Queux
W. Makepeace Thackeray
William W. Walter
William Shakespeare
Winston Churchill
Yei Theodora Ozaki
Yogi Ramacharaka
Young E. Allison
Zane Grey